Among the eminent en
in high esteem is Dr.
book, who, in one volu
losophy of life and business management he formulated through wide ranging personal experience. I am
impressed with his passion and conviction—and
with his relentless admonition throughout the book
"to believe in the infinite potential of human beings
and enjoy a truly fulfilling life by developing this
potential completely." This is a book that I recom-
mend especially to the young, who should take the
time to read through it at least once.

the late KONOSUKE MATSUSHITA

… Sony's Akio Morita and Kyocera's Kazuo Inamori
are probably more global, more innovative and more
entrepreneurial than most of their Silicon Valley
counterparts.

MICHAEL SCHRAGE,
Los Angeles Times

A PASSION
FOR SUCCESS

A PASSION FOR SUCCESS

Practical, Inspirational, and Spiritual Insight from Japan's Leading Entrepreneur

KAZUO INAMORI

McGraw-Hill, Inc.
New York   San Francisco   Washington, D.C.   Auckland   Bogotá
Caracas   Lisbon   London   Madrid   Mexico City   Milan
Montreal   New Delhi   San Juan   Singapore
Sydney   Tokyo   Toronto

Library of Congress Cataloging-in-Publication Data

Inamori, Kazuo, date.
    A passion for success :   practical, inspirational, and spiritual
  insight from Japan's leading entrepreneur / Kazuo Inamori.
        p.   cm.
    ISBN 0-07-031784-4
    1. Executives—Conduct of life.   2. Businessmen—Conduct
  of life.   3. Industrial management.   I. Title.
  HF5387.I5   1995
  658.4′09—dc20   95-13183
                                                                CIP

        5 6 7 8 9 0   DOC/DOC   0 0

ISBN 0-07-031784-4

*The sponsoring editor for this book was Betsy Brown, the edit-
ing supervisor was Paul R. Sobel, and the production supervisor was Pamela A. Pelton. It was set in Fairfield by Victoria
Khavkina of McGraw-Hill's Professional Book Group composi-
tion unit.*

Printed and bound by R. R. Donnelley & Sons Company.

McGraw-Hill books are available at special quantity discounts to use as
premiums and sales promotions, or for use in corporate training programs.
For more information, please write to the Director of Special Sales,
McGraw-Hill, Professional Publishing, Two Penn Plaza, New York, NY
10121-2298. Or contact your local bookstore.

Contents

EFFORT

ATTITUDE

How To Succeed In Business

SINCERITY

STRENGTH

INNOVATION

Introduction

I owe my success to having a "philosophy."

In fact, Kyoto Ceramic, Ltd. was originally funded by a man who mortgaged his house because he liked my "philosophy"! He asked just one thing from me:

"Never be a slave to money."

But in my mind I made another promise: to repay my debt to that man as soon as possible. Kyocera became profitable by the end of its first year, and has remained profitable every year since.

By 1971, we were ready to go public. I was eager to repay Mr. Nishieda, our benefactor, for his investment—but he insisted that it was not necessary. Seeing my puzzled expression, he explained:

I did not invest in you to become rich. I did it because of your philosophy. If you take your company public, you will have more shareholders—more owners—and it will not be as easy for you to manage this company in your own way.

I have now written this book to share with you what I have gained through this *philosophy*: how it helped me in my personal life, how it helped us build our business, and how I believe it can help U.S.-Japan relations and world peace by promoting harmony and prosperity.

A PASSION
FOR SUCCESS

HOW TO SUCCEED IN LIFE

A
FORMULA
FOR
SUCCESS

*Write yourself a starring role
in the drama called Life.*

❧ The Drama Called Life ❧

Life is a drama in which each one of us plays our own starring role. But in the drama of our own lives, we do more than simply act—we actually write the script. Unlike a play which must lead to a predetermined conclusion, the outcomes of our lives are in our own hands.

Some people believe that our lives are determined by destiny at birth. I disagree. I believe that our destiny can be altered by raising our minds and our way of thinking.

Instead of fighting our "destiny," we should shape our minds to write our own script for the starring role we wish to play. The sooner we do, the sooner we can start living every moment of every day to its fullest by taking control of our own lives.

Opportunities await us at every corner of life. If we are striving for a chance, we can seize them. But unless we have a clear mission and purpose in mind, we will miss even the most obvious and extraordinary prospects.

In the drama of life, there is a huge difference between those who have written themselves a starring role, and those who idle through life without aim.

ஜ Learn from Your Elders ஜ

When we were young, we tended to defy our parents, teachers, and elders when they tried to teach us about life. My own parents had a favorite saying: "The young should experience adversity even if we have to *buy* it." And I had a favorite response: "The young should *never* experience adversity, even if we have to *sell* it!"

We all go through stages of rebellion in our adolescence. But we should never forget what our parents and elders have taught us.

Starting the journey of life on our own is like rowing a boat onto an ocean without a compass.

As we mature, we should be prepared to recall what we have learned from our elders and use these lessons as a compass to guide our lives.

My philosophy, I hope, will serve a similar purpose. Some people might feel defiant or uninterested in what I say. But when you encounter obstacles in your life or career, you will need some type of value system to guide your decision making.

I learned every element of my own philosophy through the trials of my work, worries of my life, and serious, in-depth thinking. I believe that sooner or later you, too, will experience similar situations in your life.

❧ Seek a Purpose in Life ❧

More and more individuals, especially young people, seem to have lost their purpose in life. They live from one moment to the next, seeking immediate gratification. Their sole purpose for working is to earn a paycheck in the hope of "finding themselves" in leisure and entertainment.

Such a pursuit of happiness will be futile.

An "easy" lifestyle may initially seem carefree and pleasurable, but sooner or later, we all crave a higher purpose in life.

Regardless of the era in which we live, the essence of a human being remains the same. It is to seek goodness in life and achieve "immortality" by leaving something worthwhile to posterity. We should seek a life that is fulfilling, so we can one day say "I worked hard, I made worthy contributions, and I am happy."

Some people may disagree with me on this idea, but I sincerely believe that this earnest way of life is better than the "easy" way. People with more experience may understand what I am talking about. Unfortunately, they are often reluctant to share their own views on life. Their usual excuse is that times have changed and their old stories are just not relevant to today's youth. But if we speak from the heart, most people will come to share our beliefs.

See Yourself as You Are

Could it be that we humans are not as smart as we think we are?

I am old enough now to look back on my life objectively. When I do, I find many regrets. "Why did I do it *that* way?" is a recurring question. Better decisions seem obvious in retrospect.

As children, when we were about to make a poor decision, our parents would go out of their way to warn us of the problems that could result. Though they were wise, they too must have had many regrets as they looked back on their own lives. In fact, our parents' advice probably came from a desire to spare us from the mistakes that caused them pain in *their* youth.

Generations come and go, yet the same human mistakes are continually repeated.

If we could foresee the future, we could plan our lives to make all the right moves at the right times. However, it is often these mistakes themselves that give us the maturity to face life's challenges.

To improve ourselves, we must have the humility and honesty to look at ourselves objectively—and the self-discipline to learn from past mistakes.

❧ Succeed One Step at a Time ❧

Many young people have dreams of accomplishing great deeds in their lives. We should encourage *all* youth to have such dreams. However, they must also learn that great deeds can be accomplished only through daily hard work.

> *Without effort, a great vision will remain just an unfulfilled dream. No worthwhile goal has ever been attained without strenuous, meaningful labor.*

In the journey of life, there is no magic carpet. We must walk on our own two feet, one step at a time. It may seem impossible to cover great distances using this slow and deliberate method. You may begin to believe that you will never achieve anything great at such a pace—yet you must remain patient.

The accumulation of your small steps has a compounding effect. Daily, tedious effort produces little victories that urge you on to even greater efforts. These increased efforts also bring greater results, and the compounding effect can raise you up to incredible heights if you simply *keep going*.

In our personal lives or in managing a business, "one step at a time" is the only sure way to make a dream come true.

❧ Live by a Formula for Success ❧

How can an average person become a remarkable success? The answer lies in a simple equation:

$$\text{The Result of Your Life} = \text{Ability} \times \text{Effort} \times \text{Attitude}$$

Your *abilities*—health, talents, and innate aptitudes—may largely be hereditary. However, the degree of *effort* you expend in life depends upon your strong desire. I rate both ability and effort on a scale from 0 to 100. As we immerse ourselves in our work, these two factors are multiplied together.

Thus, people of average ability, who realize their shortcomings and try very hard to compensate for them, may actually outperform those who are naturally gifted who have grown accustomed to not working especially hard.

Yet the third element is the *attitude* of how we live and work. And it is the most important of the three—for it can be ranked from -100 to $+100$. If a person is steeped in jealousy, resentment, or hatred, his or her attitude will be negative—and so will the outcome of his or her life. In contrast, the more positive and determined a person is, the more successful his or her life will be.

This formula illustrates that the outcomes of our lives are largely in our own hands, and that our philosophy greatly determines our personal and professional success.

A Conversation with Kazuo Inamori on the Formula for Success

What is the origin of the following formula?

$$\text{Success} = \text{Ability} \times \text{Effort} \times \text{Attitude}$$

When some colleagues and I decided to start our own company, we realized that we were just ordinary, young engineers with very little business experience. I came up with the "formula for success" to convince them that we could be successful even with our limited ability—which was, indeed, no more than average. We had to have the right philosophy and the zeal to work harder than other, more gifted people.

Why are the three factors in your formula multiplied rather than added?

If the three factors were added, this formula would suggest that gifted people have a real edge over normal people without even lifting a finger. It would indicate that those of us who are average should have difficulty competing with them through sheer hard work and effort. But because these factors are multiplied together, positive attitude and passionate effort assume a much higher level of importance. This is reality. It is indeed possible for a normal, everyday person to work hard and produce a better result than someone else who is truly gifted—perhaps even a genius—given the right attitude and passion.

Also, even a hard-working genius would produce nothing significant if he or she ran around in circles without a clear direction in life. Worse yet, some sociopaths with superior abilities have worked hard to mastermind major crimes. If one's attitude is negative, the entire result becomes negative.

Of the three, ability, effort, and attitude, which is the most important?

In talking with many managers, I find that most of them agree with my concept of ability and effort. Ironically, it is easy to forget attitude, which I consider to be the most important of the three. There is nothing more dangerous than a hard-working genius with a criminal mind.

When I graduated from college, it was very difficult to find a job in Japan. I applied to many, many companies, but no one would hire me. Frustrated, I thought perhaps I should become a "Robin Hood" type of outlaw. Since this world was so unfair and unequal, it would be better to be a Robin Hood who would take from the rich and distribute wealth among the poor.

If I had remained in that frame of mind, I might now be a gang leader. That's because I have some ability and a lot of enthusiasm and determination to succeed. However, since my philosophy would have been negative from the start, the outcome of my life would have been negative as well.

ABILITY

*The greatest ability of all is the ability
to overcome one's self.*

❧ Admit What You Cannot Do ❧

When I landed my first job in April 1955, I was a true country bumpkin. I had never lived in a large city and I spoke with a heavy southern accent. Every time a phone rang, I hoped someone else would answer it. I did not want to reveal my provincial dialect, and I really felt handicapped.

But instead of developing an inferiority complex, I decided to accept my imperfections and strive to overcome them so I would not have to feel like a failure.

"I am a country bumpkin," I admitted to myself. "I attended a back-country college. I know nothing about the world and lack common sense. I cannot expect to succeed unless I learn everything from scratch and work harder than everyone else."

In short, I learned not to deny my weaknesses. By accepting them as real, I did not have to pretend. I was free to take further steps to improve.

Don't pretend you can do what you really can't.
Admit what you cannot do and start from there.

That was the lesson I learned when I joined Shofu Industries, a small company in Kyoto. I have been reminded of it many times throughout my life.

&. Force Yourself to Excel &.

Under our current school system, a student with a "C" average who studies just enough to pass can graduate just like someone who studies intensely and achieves straight "A's." However, the difference between these two people is much greater than just two letter grades. To excel, the "A" student had to break through many barriers—some of which must have required excruciating efforts to overcome.

Whether we settle for "passing grades" or constantly challenge ourselves to be the very best is more than a matter of academics. It is an opportunity to demonstrate our human qualities and select the path we want to follow in life.

If you wish to excel in life, you must be willing to encounter many barriers. The biggest of all is your own mind, which seeks comfort and ease.

Self-denial leads you to overcome barriers and excel. It is hard to drive ourselves forward, because we naturally prefer the easy way. But knowing this makes our joy even greater when we do see our efforts come to fruition.

The greatest skill of all is the ability to overcome oneself.

❧ Overcome Yourself ❧

We all know two types of students. The first type is not necessarily very smart but works hard in school to graduate with honors. The second type is characterized by the highly intelligent playboy who breezes through college without cracking a book. The latter would say, "That bookworm got high grades—but if I had studied like he did, he would have been no match for me."

After graduation, the playboy runs into another friend who is successful in business, and observes, "He was mediocre in school. My grades were far superior to his," sinuating that if he were in his friend's shoes, he would have done better.

But is it really so? To be a bookworm is to overcome that part of oneself which seeks immediate gratification—not spending time partying or even watching television. The successful friend has probably made similar sacrifices. He has had to restrain his desire to have fun and devoted himself completely to his work. It takes great strength to overcome oneself. When we consider a person's ability, we should include his or her willpower. If someone has lost the struggle with self and decided to take the easy way, his or her total ability is indeed sharply curtailed.

Our ability to succeed throughout the long journey of life does not depend on intelligence alone.

❧ Be Bold *and* Sensitive ❧

In general, there are two types of people: the accurate, sensitive, methodical introvert; and the daring, bold, outgoing extrovert. Like a cloth woven with vertical and horizontal threads, a person needs both extremes to succeed in business.

In samurai dramas, the Japanese version of American Westerns, we see a swordsman who may outwardly look sloppy or even drunk. Yet, he can recognize enemy footsteps sneaking up behind him. He slashes the would-be attacker over his shoulder without even looking back. We applaud his skill. And in his seemingly bold actions, we can see razor-sharp sensitivity.

The irony is this: with boldness alone, you cannot do a perfect job. Yet with only sensitivity, you will not be courageous enough to challenge new things. At work, we need a person who has the contradictory characteristics of boldness and accuracy, and who knows how to use each properly in different situations. I believe that an ideal person is someone who is inherently sensitive and razor sharp, and has acquired real courage through wide-ranging experience.

Not many people are born this way. Through conscious effort, however, those of us who tend toward either extreme can achieve a greater balance.

Strive to develop ways of complementing your
inborn proclivity for either boldness or sensitivity.

≈ Master Your Instincts ≈

Human beings are born with both "instinct" and "intellect." Eating, drinking, fighting, and feeling possessive or jealous are all part of the self-preservation instinct by which we protect our lives and propagate our families. We often make decisions by using our instincts as a basis of judgment; however, animals behave in much the same way. Better decisions may come if we look at the situation objectively.

It is important to master your instincts. This will create some space in your mind where intellect can grow and allow you to reason logically. What matters is just how much of your behavior is controlled by intellect alone.

It is not easy to master our instincts. We cannot live without them, and I am not advocating that we get rid of them altogether. The important thing is not to be *ruled* by them. We need the ability to control our instincts at will.

Since humans tend to follow their instincts by nature, this challenge can be extremely difficult. There is no simple way to do this. We need to catch our selfish desires as soon as they emerge and use our intellect to suppress them.

You must learn to control your instincts. This will develop your intellect and give you the ability to make the right decisions.

❧ Focus Your Intellect ❧

The intellect is the rational part of your mind which reasons and judges. In order to use your intellect, you have to focus it as though you were collecting sunlight through a lens to start a fire. In Japanese, this conscious focusing is called voluntary attention, or *yuui chuui*. In contrast, when our awareness is instinctive—when we respond spontaneously to a loud noise, for example—it is considered involuntary attention.

As humans, we can train our intellect. If we exercise our voluntary attention for many years, we will develop the ability to focus it like a laser beam. The minute a need arises, our intellect will start functioning, penetrating to the core of any problem.

Ultimately, as we learn to free ourselves from our instincts and selfish desires, a mental power with an even greater acuity than the intellect may appear. It is called *inspiration*. It is quick, accurate, and decisive, and it requires no deliberate analysis or speculation. Great figures in history have accomplished remarkable deeds through inspiration, yet we understand little about how or why it occurs.

Today, at critical moments in our daily struggles, an idea may flash into our minds like a Divine revelation. I believe this to be an "inspiration" which is given to us when we are fully immersed in our work, bravely facing adversity, and questioning what is the right thing to do as human beings.

❧ Project Your Ability ❧

When choosing a long-term goal, I purposely select something beyond my ability.

In other words, I choose a goal which is impossible for me to accomplish *at the present time*: no matter how hard I struggle now, I will not be able to reach it. Then I set a date in the future by which time I shall have achieved it.

To reach such a goal, team leaders must plan to raise their abilities and those of their teams to the necessary level. In other words, the group doesn't simply plan to achieve a goal. We plan to develop the necessary skills and abilities *required* to achieve that goal.

Anyone can tell what he can or cannot do today by judging his present capability—but this is not sufficient to accomplish something new. An earth-shaking result can be produced only from efforts to achieve something that, at the present time, is obviously impossible.

A person who wants to accomplish something new and worthwhile must assess his or her own ability from both present and future viewpoints.

ಶ Build Your Character ಶ

Small business owners are often full of spirit—with sharp eyes for business opportunities, extraordinary talent, and extremely shrewd business acumen. In many cases, however, they are unyielding.

Most businesses can operate adequately on sheer talent and ability. However, these alone are not always enough to keep a business from failing. Small business owners tend to dive into ventures one after another, relying only on their talents to achieve their goals. Yet, even if they succeed temporarily, their business will be unstable if they become trapped by their own abilities.

Without sufficient strength of soul, we can easily become a slave to our own talents.

There are, on the other hand, people who make their ability serve them. Their virtuous and respectable "self" controls their ability. The dominant actor in this drama must be the "self."

Few people are born with a virtuous personality. Initially we depend on our talent, business ability, and fighting spirit to succeed. However, to turn our business into a lifetime mission, we must elevate our minds and build a virtuous character within ourselves.

A Conversation with Kazuo Inamori on Ability

Are leaders born or trained?

I have often pondered the same question. I think the answer is "both." Just as there are natural athletes, musicians, or artists, there are people born with natural ability for leadership and charisma. However, I also believe that almost all people can train themselves to be good, if not outstanding, leaders.

What is more important than ability is the effort leaders make and the fundamental truths and principles upon which their leadership is based. The most tragic case is a competent leader with a negative way of thinking who leads his or her group astray or into self-destruction.

EFFORT

*Today's impossibility becomes
tomorrow's reality
when human efforts are fueled by
enthusiasm and passion.*

❧ Why Work? ❧

What is the meaning of work?

Everyone must earn a living to support themselves and their families. But what if you were born so rich that you did not need to work? We all enjoy occasional leisure time. But if you had to idle your time away every day, eventually you would become unbearably bored. It appears that there is more to work than simply earning a paycheck.

Work can provide a degree of spiritual satisfaction. In fact, we may discover new meaning in life through our work.

But work is hard. Work requires long periods of concentrated effort. Work can be quite arduous. And, if we work solely out of obligation, it only becomes harder. It is virtually intolerable to work for years strictly out of a sense of duty.

We must change our arduous work into something that is worth living for. How can we do this? We might start by telling ourselves that we *enjoy* our work. Through conscious efforts, we can guide our minds into looking at work positively.

Whether or not we have a job to which we can devote ourselves throughout life will determine how happy or unhappy we may be. But first, we must find meaning in work.

❧ Break through the Wall ❧

The line between a successful person and an unsuccessful person is paper thin. In fact, people who do not succeed are not necessarily irresponsible; many are sincere, enthusiastic, and hardworking, just like those who achieve remarkable goals.

And yet, some succeed while others fail. You might think society is unfair. But between these two groups of people is a barrier—a wall that is paper thin, yet difficult to penetrate.

The difference is tenacity and perseverance. When unsuccessful people face a brick wall, they assume it is impenetrable. This is common sense. In other words, they do make an effort, but with limitations. When they run into a wall, they find commonsense reasons to excuse themselves and resign.

Even when a task seems impossible, we must tenaciously and diligently persevere in our efforts to succeed. We have to destroy the "conventional wisdom" that is fixed within our minds. Any stubborn preconceptions regarding our own limitations will hinder us from crossing the line to success.

The self-confidence and pride in finally breaking through a barrier will make your personality stronger and more tenacious, and this tenacity will lead you to another, greater success.

❧ Open a New Era ❧

Some people give numerous reasons why they cannot achieve something—a lack of this or that; they always have a reason. But if we all thought this way, nobody would ever achieve anything new.

You should begin every new project by assuming you are starting with nothing. Accept this as a fact. Then develop the desire to accomplish your project *no matter what*. Create a plan that shows clearly how to reach your goal—including how you will acquire the necessary staff, funds, equipment, and techniques. Then, I believe, you can make your dream come true.

Untold hardships and difficulties await everyone who embarks on a new business project. To succeed, you must acknowledge this, believe in yourself, and pursue your goal with a desperate desire.

You may be asked about the probability of your success, and you may not know the answer, but it does not matter. The world of creativity is governed not by statistics, but by the passion and will of the designer!

In any revolution, passion is what opens new eras.

❧ Love Your Job ❧

You may be thinking about quitting your job right now.

To be frank, there are times when I do, too. I feel burned out. It reminds me of school: I spent long nights agonizing over exams until I just wanted to run away. And even now, I still occasionally feel the same way.

But I don't really believe that quitting your job will turn your life into paradise. If I did quit, I would probably be eager to go back to work within three days.

People tell me that I lead an arduous life. But despite all the anxieties I have, I find my life meaningful. I do love my work. Nonetheless, every so often I feel exhausted with the responsibility of my position.

We occasionally see people who seem to be enduring an unimaginable hardship. But if those people really enjoy their work, they probably will not even remember it as a hardship.

Only people who love their work and find foremost enjoyment in their jobs will succeed in business.

To be truly successful and achieve great results,
we must first fall in love with our work.

❧ Concentrate on One Thing ❧

I truly believe that a person can find truth in life and even understand the universe by concentrating on one thing and mastering it.

For example, I know a carpenter who has devoted himself to his craft for years. He has attained superior skills and can also tell remarkable stories about life. A monk who has disciplined himself and elevated his own character can often teach great truths even in completely unrelated fields. People who have worked hard to master any skill—painting, welding, writing, whatever—can share similar insights.

Unfortunately, young people graduating from school quickly grow impatient with their unglamorous, entry-level jobs. They wonder if their work will ever lead to anything meaningful, and they plead for different responsibilities—but they may never be satisfied.

The saying, "Jack of all trades, master of none" contains an element of truth. If our knowledge is broad but shallow, we really know nothing. Yet pursuing one skill or field in great depth can illuminate the universe.

Mastering one subject can bring tremendous understanding, for deep inside every fact lies the truth which governs all.

❧ Open Your Own Path ❧

Sometimes misfortune is a blessing in disguise.

When I took my first job at a small company in Kyoto, circumstances were extremely unpleasant. The paychecks were late, no bonus was awarded, and I began to lose hope in my future with that company.

I seriously considered quitting. But my brother, Toshinori, scolded and dissuaded me, reminding me that jobs were scarce and that my family needed my financial support. I had no choice. I *had* to stay with that company. So I decided to change what I could control—myself. I decided to change my attitude, find joy in my work, and carve my way out of those dire circumstances.

I began to devote myself to research, with outstanding results. The company did not have exceptionally brilliant personnel, so I was able to stand out. My supervisor praised me. That encouraged me to work harder, leading to more praise. From that point on, my life seemed to open up to new opportunities.

Had I been blessed with better jobs and working conditions from the start, I might not have had the opportunity to accomplish what I have.

You can discern the true blessings in your life only if you are open to them.

❧ Sound Mind, Sound Body ❧

"A sound mind in a sound body" is a saying that dates back to the Roman empire, yet its meaning remains timely even today.

If you want to be a leader, you must make an effort to maintain your health. When you, as the head of a group, make decisions, those decisions must not be influenced by any matters relating to your own personal health.

Poor health may affect your decision-making ability, preventing you from choosing a direction that would require a lot of physical stamina or endurance. And even if this influence is subconscious, it could lead to imprudent decisions that ultimately bring unhappiness to a great number of people.

To be frank, I think leaders should resign when health considerations might cause their decisions to be impaired. However, these people can still help the group from staff positions by sharing their many years of experience and knowledge.

You must make an effort to cultivate a sound body for your sound mind, for a leader must be fair, impartial, and able to make unselfish decisions.

❧ Live a Contrite Life ❧

What I mean by a "contrite life" is a life where I am constantly and sincerely reviewing myself, questioning whether I am doing what is right as a human being, and trying to exercise self-discipline in my behavior. I try to be collected and humble in my reflections. And, when I see any vestige of self-ishness or cowardice, I say, "Stop thinking only of yourself," or "Have the courage to do what you know is right." As I repeat this practice, I become more keenly aware of my own heart in ways that allow me to avoid bad judgments and potential mistakes.

We all know of people who were self-disciplined in youth and achieved great success, only to become arrogant in later years to the point that old friends remark, "Success has ruined him." Our human nature is eager to let us rest on our laurels. Unfortunately, no matter how successful we are in elevating ourselves, we may lose all we have gained unless we strive to remain humble, reflect upon our hearts, and learn every day.

People like us, who work relentlessly, tend to end each day merely completing tasks and not reflecting upon ourselves. But if we intend to elevate our human qualities, we must reflect critically on the reality of what we are and the ideal of how we should be.

If we fail to live a contrite life, success itself can be our downfall.

❧ Let Good Books Expand Your Horizon ❧

Instead of reading for enjoyment only, I believe we should all read to elevate and refine ourselves. We should make it a habit to find good books and seriously absorb what is in them.

I always read after coming home from work or entertaining customers, even late at night. And I don't sit at a desk. I read in my bedroom, where I keep a lot of classical literature and books on philosophy.

I even read in the bathtub. And when I have a weekend off, I love to spend the day reading books.

You may feel too busy to spare any time reading. Still, it is always possible to take a few moments out of your limited schedule, wherever you may be, to open a good book and be deeply touched by the content.

Of course, the most important lessons in life are those we learn through *experience.* But reading offers a reference point that can make these experiences more meaningful. Further, books offer a mental "simulation" which can teach us about experiences we may never have the chance to acquire.

Your own experiences and those of others that you acquire through reading can provide a spiritual framework to succeed in life.

❧ Infuse Your Energy into Others ❧

Leaders need subordinates to accomplish what they cannot do alone. Yet even if you are *burning* with passion, you will have difficulty making your project succeed if your subordinates do not share the same zeal.

You may assign your employees to the best project imaginable and provide the finest resources. Unless your team members become "fired up," however, the project will not succeed.

On the other hand, if you can communicate your goals passionately and raise the spirit of your team as high as your own, success will be possible even when material resources are lacking. Infuse your energy into theirs and create a single force. This will raise the team's energy level even higher than your own.

If subordinates merely agree to work on your project, there is probably a 30 percent chance that you will succeed. If they say, "I'll do my best," perhaps there is a 50 percent chance. But if you can infuse your energy into them so they consider your project to be *theirs,* I would say you have a 90 percent chance of success.

Finding out how passionate your subordinates are about their jobs, and infusing your energy into them until they burn with passion, are the most important duties of a leader.

❧ Live One Earnest Day at a Time ❧

I don't make any long-term business plans. When we don't even know how our work will turn out today, or what tomorrow holds in store, how can we foresee conditions 10 years down the road?

Instead, I tell myself to *live each day earnestly.* If I work hard and try to improve things, maybe I will be able to envision tomorrow. A series of individual days will then accumulate into a big result five or ten years from now.

It is more important for me to live earnestly today than to worry about an uncertain future. I believe this firmly enough to have made it a guiding principle of my research and management.

As a result, I can honestly say that if we live earnestly today, we will be able to envision tomorrow with a fair degree of accuracy. This has helped me to understand how certain trends will develop and continue in the future.

An old proverb states that, "By mastering one thing completely, you gain access to all things."

Similarly, if we live each day earnestly, we will be able to acquire bits of universal knowledge. The only way to *predict* our future with any degree of accuracy is to make it an extension of our efforts today.

A Conversation with Kazuo Inamori on Effort

People say that you have a knack for succeeding at almost any major project you undertake. How do you do it?

Very simply, I do not give up until I am satisfied with a project. Failure is a state of mind. I don't start a major project unless I am thoroughly convinced that it is truly worthwhile. Then I don't have a reason to give it up when I encounter an obstacle. If one way is not successful, I can search for another until I find a way to get to the true goal behind the project. Sometimes I have to be patient.

How do you treat workers who are unproductive?

We all have differences in ability. Some workers are extremely capable and other workers are less so. As long as workers remain positive and make sincere efforts, managers should treat them well, regardless of their ability to contribute. Managers need to identify workers' strengths and find a place in the organization where they can contribute more.

What do you do with workers who have a negative attitude?

When we find workers who have a negative attitude, we try to talk to them. We try to show how essential a positive attitude is for us as individuals as well as for the company. In an extreme case, we may even suggest that they find another company or occupation where they can feel more positive and, thus, productive. Those workers who continue to have a negative attitude tend to leave the company naturally after a while.

Do you think long-term plans are unnecessary?

Throughout my life, I have always believed that the best way to predict the future is to work earnestly every day and to look at tomorrow as the extension of our daily efforts. In other words, if you want tomorrow to turn out as you hope it will, you must work hard today and accomplish what you set out to do. Individual managers have their own style of management. What I shared about not making long-term business plans describes my own management style. In the case of Kyocera, we mostly rely upon our yearly master plans. I believe it is important to have a vision of where we are heading. But a long-term plan will make us into liars as often as it may make us look like prophets.

ATTITUDE

Greed will complicate even
the simplest problems;
a selfless way of thinking
leads to true success.

❧ Never Lose Hope ❧

Nowadays, I believe that our lives will turn out exactly as we imagine they will. But when I first started working, that idea was the furthest from my mind. Everything I did was going wrong.

Somehow, I never lost my hope and cheerfulness—and I think that made me what I am today.

Back then I lived on the second floor of a ramshackle dormitory in a 10-foot by 10-foot room with a *tatami* (straw mat) floor. The tatami mats were threadbare and had lost their covers, so shabby straws were sticking out. I had a portable charcoal stove and a pot, and cooked my own meals every day.

The research at work was going badly. So were my relationships with others. At dusk I used to go to a little stream lined with blooming cherry trees behind the dormitory. And I would sit down on the bank and sing the song *Furusato* (the name of my home village). My heart was aching from many wounds and I didn't know what to do to soothe the pain. I tried to keep up my spirits by singing aloud. I sang until it gave me the courage to return to my room and reapply myself at work the next day.

We can never be completely free from anguish and worry. But even in your worst moment, try not to lose your cheerfulness and hope for tomorrow.

❧ Seek Righteousness ❧

I learned as a youth to always ask myself, "What is the right thing *for a human being* to do?"

When I had to face a harsh reality in society, I tried to say to myself "That is not humane—ideally, it should be different!" I eventually decided that the mind which seeks righteousness should also be a mind which pursues the ideal.

In my youth, I failed the entry examinations for the schools of my choice. I did not get the jobs I applied for. I met disappointment. But I responded by making greater efforts. When I was assigned to perform obscure research to develop a new type of ceramics, I told myself I should try my best to make ceramics a superb material.

Under seemingly hopeless adversity, I tried to keep up my ideals and my spirits, and I worked hard to realize my dreams.

In your long journey of life, you will experience many disappointments, difficulties, and trying times. But those are the opportunities for you to really make a sincere effort—and with all the strength you can muster, to leap toward your dreams.

Heaven will not ignore sincere effort and true determination.

❧ Avoid the Easy Way ❧

Upon graduation, I started working for a small ceramics company. There, I alternately clashed with management and was attacked by the labor union. I became helplessly isolated. I imagined leading my team up a tall, jagged mountain. We could have been daunted, we might have flinched or perhaps even slipped and fallen off the edge.

A senior manager urged me to compromise. It was like asking me to take a gentler path and climb the mountain slowly with the group.

I reflected upon his advice, but chose the steeper path instead. I knew that if I chose the easier way and climbed slowly, I would probably give up before reaching the summit. I knew I was a weak person. But my people trusted me. My choosing the easy way would have also made it easier for them. But that would not have led us to true happiness.

I made up my mind. Since I firmly believed this was the right path, I decided to climb it straight to the summit no matter how jagged it might become or what harsh climate I might encounter. Since then, I have always tried to be as strict with myself as with others, so that we could all reach each summit together.

The easy way does not usually lead us to our goal. I have never gone wrong believing this.

❧ Heaven or Hell? ❧

A young Buddhist monk once asked a wise priest to describe hell. The old priest replied that in hell, there is a giant cooking pot, a yard wide, filled with delicious noodles—however, your only serving utensils are chopsticks which are also a yard in length.

"You can imagine what happens," the priest explained. "Everybody is hungry and fighting to feed themselves with the yard-long chopsticks. They manage to pick noodles up, but the chopsticks are too long to maneuver the noodles into their mouths. They become frantic and flounder at the noodles, each wanting to be the first to eat, and they even attack others for their food. In the end, with noodles everywhere but in their mouths, they suffer a permanent, agonizing hunger."

The young monk then asked for a description of heaven, to which the old priest replied: "Heaven is actually quite the same. Only there, each person picks up the noodles and offers them to someone on the other side of the pot, saying 'Please be the first to enjoy this wonderful meal.' And the other accepts the food, saying, 'Thank you, and please allow me to return you the kindness.' Through their unselfish minds, they enjoy eternal bliss."

Business relationships can be heaven or hell, depending on whether we view them as win-lose situations, zero-sum games, or win-win opportunities of compounding synergy.

🍂 Trust from Within 🍂

One cannot be successful without trustworthy human relationships, especially in managing a business.

The question is, how do you go about building business relationships with others you can trust? I personally decided to start by making friends I could trust. I figured that I needed to find trustworthy relationships outside of myself.

However, I was wrong. I soon realized that I could not have a truly trusting relationship unless I first made *myself* trustworthy. Unless I could be trusted by others in the first place, I could not attract people of a trustworthy nature. Reliable relationships, I decided, are a reflection of the thoughts in your mind.

I have been betrayed by others on more than one occasion. But I do not let that bother me. I still think I should place my complete trust in others. I keep asking myself if my heart deserves their trust. If not, I need to adjust my course of behavior.

Even if we have had bad experiences, we must continue to trust others. That's the only way to start a good relationship.

Trust can't be sought outside of ourselves; we have to seek it from within.

❧ See Things as They Are ❧

A clear and pure mind can see the truth; but a selfish mind sees only complications. For example, if we undertake a task asking "What can I gain from this?" our greed will complicate even a simple problem. Oftentimes, if we are trying to make ourselves look good, our selfish motivation will throw a simple problem out of focus and delay its solution.

We should strive to have a heart that can see things *as they truly are.* Even a simple problem can become very complicated if we let our personal desires influence it.

We need to see things as they are even when doing so appears personally disadvantageous. If we find that we have done wrong, we must admit our mistake. When we start to see things with unselfish eyes, the problem may clear up and a simple solution might even suddenly appear to us. But if we do not first abandon our egotistical nature, our eyes will cloud with a desire to seek pleasure and luxury—and the truth of the matter will remain obscured.

But seeing the truth is not enough. To uphold the truth, we must have enough courage to jump into a fire.

If we see things as they are and are willing to sacrifice ourselves, there is no real problem we cannot eventually overcome.

❧ Attention to Detail ❧

A person's ability may be measured by his or her capacity to make good decisions.

To make correct decisions, we need to have a good grasp of our own situation. Our perceptions must be acute and detailed enough to penetrate to the core of any matter.

This sensitivity results from the total concentration of our minds. But it is impossible to develop such a powerful level of concentration overnight.

Concentration is a habit. If you develop the habit of paying attention to details, you can concentrate in any situation. If you don't have this habit, your mind will have a difficult time becoming and remaining focused.

You may say that you are too busy to concentrate on details. But the time to develop this habit is when you are busy. Even if it is something you are not interested in, you should make a *conscious* effort to pay attention. This is what we call "voluntary attention," or *yuui-chuui* in Japanese.

The daily exercise of voluntary attention builds your ability to make correct decisions even in emergencies. A person who has developed this attentiveness and insight to make correct decisions swiftly is a truly "capable person."

❧ Rely on Your Subconscious Mind ❧

Your subconscious mind has the power to make complex decisions correctly and easily.

Remember the first time you drove a car? It probably was an overwhelming experience. Steering alone required conscious effort as you struggled to manage the road, oncoming traffic, approaching curves, and the many other considerations in your mind. But eventually, your subconscious mind took over. Today, your "subconscious mind" instantly assesses every situation, recalls similar patterns from your past, and moves your hands and feet automatically. You drive subconsciously.

Kouzou Masuda, the Grand Master of *sho-gi* (Japanese chess), once said, "At the climax of the game, the winning move flashed across my mind. I deliberately decided to examine all possibilities, mentally playing dozens of other moves; but in the end, I conceded that my first inspiration was correct." His subconscious mind had calculated the correct move before his conscious mind could even hypothesize it.

Dramatic events and repeated experiences leave strong impressions in our subconscious minds, where they can be recalled later with amazing speed and accuracy.

The earnest repetition of tasks trains our subconscious minds to swiftly make correct decisions.

❧ Follow Your Philosophy ❧

In English we say, "It makes sense." In Japanese, we say "It has *suji*."

Suji literally means "spine" or "line." We use it to mean a line of reasoning, or "philosophy," that a person uses in making decisions. We may even say it is an index of human spirituality.

We are all called to make decisions based upon our own individual criteria. These decision criteria should be based upon sound truths and principles, such as the morality and ethics that answer to *"What is the right thing for me, as a human being, to do?"*

To judge whether something has *suji* or makes sense, we should not just ask if it is logical. Rather, we should make certain that it is in line with what we believe to be the human way. Before we agree lightheartedly that an idea makes sense, we should seriously reflect on its relevance to our basic human values. We need to see if its *suji* still makes sense.

People who lack *suji* will not be able to achieve anything worthwhile, because they will not have a sound rationale on which to base their decisions. Those with *suji* can succeed by using it as a compass to guide themselves and convince others of their beliefs.

An inner compass can lead us to correct decision-making.

❧ Truths and Principles ❧

We should always base our judgment and conduct on fundamental truths and principles.

Do not rely upon conventional wisdom and tradition in making decisions. If you do, you will be hopelessly lost when you encounter a new situation where common sense and tradition no longer apply.

If our decision making is based on universal principles and rules, no situation will perplex us.

Relying upon fundamental *truths* and *principles* means carrying a standard of righteousness as a human being which is based on human morals and ethics. If your judgment is based on human principles and righteousness, it will be accepted in any situation, regardless of time or place. A person who has the right standard of judgment could jump into an unknown world and not be perplexed.

The reason true innovators are able to open up or develop new fields is neither that they have an abundance of experience nor that they have common sense. It is that they look at the true spiritual nature of humankind, and base their decisions on fundamental principles and rational truths.

A Conversation with Kazuo Inamori on Attitude

Do you find differences in motivation and attitude between American workers and those in Japan?

We really have not deviated from our Kyocera management philosophy since we came to the United States. As we practice the same Kyocera methods, we pretty much get the same reactions from all workers.

It is true that in the United States we frequently run into workers who are more individualistic. But this is often a good thing. Americans are willing to be different, and there is always a place for more creativity in a good company. Also, American employees tend to see the merit of an idea separately from that idea's "nationality."

Do you think American managers are more self-centered?

Once in a while we do run into a manager whose individualism is more self-oriented, but we also have such people in Japan, as well as in any other country. Regardless of a person's nationality, when we are sincere and try to communicate from our heart, even the most self-centered people seem to understand and accept our way of thinking. The fact that we originated many of our management systems in Japan does not make a wrong concept acceptable, or a good idea unattractive.

Do you have a technique for involving your subconscious mind in the solution of difficult problems?

I am not an expert in this subject and I am familiar with it only from my own personal experience. But, when I become passionate and concentrate, I can benefit from my subconscious mind. Things that happened in the past that I have almost forgotten are brought to my attention. I do not have a special method except to be passionately immersed in the subject. Perhaps this is not the most efficient technique, but this is the way I know—and it seems to work for me.

HOW TO
SUCCEED
IN BUSINESS

PASSION *for Success*

The seven letters of the word *PASSION* represent the initials of seven essential principles of management:

- **PROFIT.** Maximize sales and minimize expenses; instead of pursuing profit, let profit follow you.

- **AMBITION.** Nurture your ambition continuously until it penetrates into your subconscious mind.

- **SINCERITY.** Think about the other party in all your business transactions; aim for a win-win situation.

- **STRENGTH.** True strength is courage; never act in a cowardly manner.

- **INNOVATION.** Today should be better than yesterday; tomorrow, better than today. Use your individual creativity to achieve continuous improvement.

- **OPTIMISM.** Always maintain a positive, cheerful disposition; have a pure mind that is filled with hopes and dreams.

- **NEVER GIVE UP.** Work harder than anybody else; perform even the most tedious work steadily, without relenting in your effort.

In this section, we shall see how these seven articles of management are tied together with the same underlying motivation—the "passion" for success.

ᶎ The Drama Called "Enterprise" ᶎ

I regard a company as a theatrical troupe of sorts which performs a drama called "Enterprise."

Many different roles are needed to stage a drama. A famous actor and actress may play starring roles. And there are protagonists, heroes, villains, and enemies. The backstage crew, musicians, and electricians all work together to produce the play.

All human beings are equal; these actors merely have different roles.

If the stars wore stagehands' work clothes, the drama probably wouldn't make sense. Actors and actresses have to dress and act their part. And, so it is with a company. Being the president is just a role. If the chief executive officer is shabbily dressed, the company's image may suffer. Officers also receive certain privileges that are commensurate with their responsibilities, because it is their role. However, this does not permit them to be opportunistic or take advantage of others—that would constitute an abuse of authority.

The quality of a company reflects the passion for excellence that each member of the cast displays. While the roles may differ, each actor or actress is a professional in his or her own right.

❧ Passion Leads to Success ❧

When I evaluate anyone, I consider that person's talent and ability. But I believe it is equally important to consider the passion that person possesses.

That's because if you have passion, you can accomplish almost anything.

If you don't have ability, but have passion, you can arrange to have capable people around you. Even if you don't have funds or facilities, people will respond to your dreams if you allow your passion to persuade them.

Your passion is the source of success and accomplishment; the stronger your will, enthusiasm, and passion for success, the better your chance to succeed.

Passion is a state in which you think of something 24 hours a day, even as you sleep. In reality, it is impossible to keep thinking consciously 24 hours a day. However, it is important to maintain such an intention. In so doing, your desire will reach your subconscious mind—which can indeed remain focused asleep or awake.

The key to success is your passion.

❧ Passion with a Pure Mind ❧

True passion can bring you success. But if the passion arises from your own greed or self-interest, the success will be short-lived. If you become insensitive to what is right for society, and start pushing ahead thinking only about yourself, the same passion which brought you success initially will cause you to fail in the end.

Ultimately, success depends on the purity of the desire that reaches our subconscious minds.

It would be ideal if we could rid ourselves of our selfishness and have completely altruistic and pure desires for humanity and society. But it is almost impossible for us, as human beings, to fully eradicate our self-interest and greed. And we should not feel ashamed of this. We need some egotistic desires as part of the self-preservation mechanism that keeps us alive. But we also need to make an effort to control them.

We should at least shift our work objective from working just for ourselves to doing so for our group. By shifting our objective away from ourselves to others, the purity of our desire will increase. Eventually, the strong desire of a pure mind will prevail.

It has often been my experience, when I am agonizing and worrying over a purely selfless desire, to suddenly see a solution to the problem. I like to think of this as a Higher Power granting me an insight by letting my desperate but pure desire reach my subconscious mind.

✿ "Amoeba" Management ✿

"To drive a car, you need to turn your starter to get your engine going," I tell my executives. Likewise, to start a major project, you need managers who share your passion and use it to motivate their employees.

When Kyocera was building its second plant, I became concerned. We were a young company, growing rapidly because of our entrepreneurial passion. But I worried that we might eventually become like any other large corporation—a bureaucracy without any pioneering passion. I wanted to raise entrepreneurs in Kyocera.

I thus divided our company into small profit centers called "amoebas." Each is a small venture business with one person acting as the leader, or nucleus. A typical amoeba buys everything it needs from outside the company or from other amoebas. It profits by selling its products and services to others or to outside customers. Each amoeba shares in the passion of the amoeba leader, and is evaluated by its *hourly efficiency*—the average added value per work-hour of its members.

Several small amoebas make up larger amoebas which, in turn, are grouped into even larger amoebas. Kyocera itself is a gigantic amoeba, composed of thousands of amoebas all over the world.

Ignite your managers with your passion, so they may ignite passion in their subordinates.

A Conversation with Kazuo Inamori on PASSION

Why is passion important?

Passion enables you to unlock the tremendous power of your subconscious mind.

At the conscious level, an ordinary person will have a difficult time competing with a genius. Most psychologists agree, however, that the power of the subconscious mind is an order of magnitude higher than that of the conscious mind. A small company, such as the newly founded Kyocera, could never expect to recruit truly extraordinary geniuses as employees. But we believe we have shown that even ordinary people can accomplish miracles if they can tap into their subconscious minds.

How does PASSION work?

Let us assume that you are out of work and need income to feed your family. You decide to start a hot dog stand. Obviously, you expect it to be *profitable.*

From the beginning, you should avoid the defeatist attitude that you are embarking on this endeavor because you lost your job and cannot find other employment. Instead, find an *ambitious* cause that will encourage you and your family. Be full of enthusiasm and hope in order to face your future as an independent entrepreneur. Share your ambition with your family and friends, along with the reasons why this is going to be worth your total efforts.

Don't be shy with your dreams. Be daring. It is not a sin to get high on big dreams. But you should make sure that your plan benefits others who will be working with you. Of course, it will be so much better if your dream benefits society. Above all, you need to be *sincere*—sincere with yourself as well as with others. You have to be sincere to be fully objective and factual.

Being factual is important as you start imagining and simulating your dream. You have to set specific objectives and targets. Imagine the process that will lead to your goal. For example, you can go through the mental process of buying a used van and converting it into a mobile hot dog stand. You can imagine yourself putting in propane gas to cook your hot dogs and a soft-drink dispenser for sodas. Then you can picture yourself driving your van to the places where you are most likely to sell your hot dogs. Will you go after college dorms, construction workers on job sites, or luncheon crowds? You may want to check out likely spots and observe the traffic.

Think of all potential handicaps and difficulties. What if it rains? What if your van breaks down? What if people don't like your hot dogs? What if you run out of supplies? What will you do on weekends and holidays? What if your supplier cannot deliver the products to you? What if a new competitor appears? Having simulated a solution to each of these difficulties will make you *strong* and give you courage later when you actually face the problem.

Continue to think of *innovative* ways to avoid pitfalls and get your customers to buy your hot dogs. You can do this every day and night. Using your head is free and will save you many headaches later.

Keep working on your plan day in and day out, even for a month or two....Then you start to "see" how many hot dogs you will be able to sell per day, what your revenues will be, and your total estimated expenses. Discount for rainy days and holidays, and compute what your profit will be. It's as if you are already in business. You can see your business unfold in front of your eyes as clearly as if you were watching a movie. You start seeing it take on its own life, in full color. You can feel the confidence build up inside you to make the project successful. You become *optimistic* about your project. That is when you are ready to start your business. I would say that your project now has a very good chance of succeeding.

Then, once you have started your business, you must have the determination and tenacity to stick to it. *Never give up* until you succeed!

This may be oversimplified, but if you substitute the hot dogs in this story with whatever product you are offering, you can apply the same principles.

How did you conceive the seven articles of management, the initials of which form the word PASSION?

As our company grew, we needed to move our managers up to positions that affected thousands of people. It was important that these executives would become successful in their positions, for otherwise our people could suffer. I had to do some soul searching to condense our management philosophy into a few important concepts that I could insist our executives follow no matter what.

The articles I consider most important happen to form the acronym, P.A.S.S.I.O.N.: *Profit, Ambition, Sincerity, Strength, Innovation, Optimism,* and *Never Giving Up.*

PROFIT

A person who can manage
a great business is
a person who can
bring profit to the customer.

Don't Chase Profit;
Let It Follow Your Efforts

- "Maximize revenues and minimize expenses" is the fundamental concept of any successful business.

- Profit is not to be chased. By continuously maximizing your revenue and minimizing your expenses, you must let profit naturally follow your effort. In other words, profit is the result of your continuous endeavor.

- The above advice may sound easy. It is not. A business reflects the person who runs it. The business develops in the way the manager wills it, and tremendous willpower and creativity are necessary to maximize revenues and minimize expenses. In other words, a strong and clear "ambition" is necessary.

‏❧ The Purpose of Business ❧

One year after I founded Kyocera, I realized that I had started something outrageous. Eight of us started the company to prove that the technology we developed could be accepted by society. But before long, several young people we had hired demanded that we guarantee their future income!

I had to seriously ponder the question, "What is an enterprise?" I was in no position to guarantee *anybody's* future livelihood, not even my own family's. Still, these employees were entrusting their future to our company. There was no way that we could betray the expectations of our employees, who were basing their lives on their jobs with us. Three days and nights of impassioned discussions made me change Kyocera's corporate mission. We shifted our priority from technology to employees.

> *Kyocera's management rationale is to provide opportunities for the material and intellectual growth of all our employees, and, through our joint effort, contribute to the advancement of society and mankind.*

Our business shall strive first to provide opportunities for our employees. Building upon this, we shall jointly contribute to the progress of technology, society, and humankind. I believe these are the only worthwhile objectives of our business.

❧ Pursue Profit Fairly ❧

Employers have to achieve profitability for the sake of their enterprise and their people.

This is nothing to be ashamed of. In the free market where the principle of free competition functions, the profit we gain is a just reward for doing business in a rightful manner. We streamline our operations to deliver high-valued products to our customers at minimal cost. Managers and workers earn profit by working hard. We should be proud of it.

However, we should not let the pursuit of profit overwhelm us. We should never succumb to the temptation to seek profit shamelessly. We must remain on the path of righteousness; we gain profit fairly through hard work to provide the quality products our customers demand.

We should never dream of making a fortune at a single stroke through underhanded means. For example, at the height of the oil crisis, some executives directed their companies to hold back their merchandise deliberately and raise prices. I wonder how many of these unscrupulous managers are still in executive offices today.

In a free market, profit is society's reward for those who serve its interests.

✌ The Essence of Business ✌

As society develops, age-old truths get lost among complex circumstances.

In managing a business, we should never forget what the essence of our business is.

Right before the first OPEC oil crisis, a land boom started in Japan. Many companies vied with one another to purchase land, expecting prices to skyrocket. Our banker, in fact, came to plead with us. He said he was delighted that we were depositing our profits with him—yet as our banker, he felt compelled to advise us that we could be making a fortune by investing in real estate!

I politely replied that our business was to make profit in the traditional way—by manufacturing products and adding value, not by speculating on land prices.

Then the oil crisis came, and most companies had their money tied up in land. Kyocera, however, was able to use its liquid assets to invest in plants and equipment. I was praised for our excellent balance sheets and my "clairvoyance." Of course, no one can foresee the future. But while others looked at the façade, I held on to basic truths and principles and adhered to what I believed was the essence of our business.

❧ Make Customers Happy ❧

It's a cliché to say that the way to a profitable business is to "make customers happy." Still, some companies misunderstand the real meaning of "profit" and run their business solely for their own benefit.

Such an attitude should never exist. The principle of business is to please people. We must certainly make our outside customers happy. And we must please our internal customers, too—the other employees and departments who depend on us.

The reason we work hard to meet a deadline is to deliver our products when our customers need them. We make state-of-the-art products to meet and exceed our customer's expectations. We continually develop new products to help our customers make more profit themselves. Everything we do in business derives from our principle of pleasing our customers.

Too many people think only of their own profit. But business opportunity seldom knocks on the door of self-centered people. No customer ever goes to a store merely to please the storekeeper.

Persons who can successfully manage a great business are those who can make their customers more profitable. This attitude will invite more business opportunities and bring profit to their own company.

❧ Pricing Is Management ❧

I tell my staff that pricing is management.

It is commonly believed that your price should be slightly below the market price to compete in the marketplace. You may lower your profit and sell as much as you can; or you can price your goods near the market price, maximize your margin, and expect to sell a lower quantity. There is an infinite choice of pricing.

In other words, we try to maximize the mathematical product of the quantity sold times the average selling price. But many factors influence sales. No simple answer is found. It is very difficult to estimate the volume of sales at any given profit margin. But, because this pricing will have such an important influence on business performance, I believe that only the top management should ultimately set prices.

In pricing, the goal is to find the maximum price customers will be happy to pay for your product. If it is too high, customers will not buy. If it is too low, customers may be happy but gross margin may be inadequate to maintain your operation no matter how much you sell. The philosophy at the top will decide the pricing. An aggressive manager will set an aggressive price while a cautious manager will price conservatively.

Pricing affects business performance. It is a reflection of management's capability and philosophy.

❧ Market-Set Pricing ❧

In pricing, I don't start from the cost accounting concept. That is, I don't establish a price by using a preset profit margin in this common formula:

Price = Cost of Goods + Overhead Costs + Profit

Generally, price is decided by the free-market mechanism. In short, the *customers* decide the price.

Since the price is decided by the market, we must continually minimize our manufacturing costs. The difference between our cost of goods and our price is the base for our gross profit. That means our effort to minimize manufacturing costs is, in fact, an effort to maximize our profit.

To minimize manufacturing costs, we should eliminate all preconceptions and common knowledge, such as worrying about the ideal percentages of material cost, labor cost, overhead expenses, and so on. We should scrutinize all areas and eliminate. any unnecessary expenses. We have to come up with the least costly method of manufacturing our product with the quality and price the market demands. In this sense, a penny saved is, indeed, a penny earned.

Maximizing profit while fully satisfying our customers' needs and desires—this is the essence of business!

❧ Follow P&L Daily ❧

You cannot successfully manage a business like a guru in seclusion, looking down on others from afar and occasionally bestowing a few words of wisdom. Instead, think of it as a slow accumulation of daily routine activities.

Managing a business, whether it is a large corporation or a small shop, is a daily accumulation of numbers. We can't manage without analyzing expenses and sales on a regular basis.

But looking at a monthly income statement to run your business is still not enough. Your monthly profit is based on the daily accumulation of operational results. Therefore, you must behave as if your profit and loss statement is being produced every day, and manage your operation accordingly.

Operating our business without paying attention to the daily figures would be like flying an airplane without looking at the instrument panel. We would lose track of where we were flying and where we were supposed to land.

The same can be said of operating a business. If we don't keep an eye on daily business operations, we will never reach our goal.

An income statement is a portrait of how the manager has behaved daily.

❧ An Unselfish Look at Profit ❧

For business executives, paying taxes is as painful as cutting our own flesh. Each year, we have to surrender more than half of the profit we worked so hard to earn. And even though some of our profits are in receivables and other noncash forms, we still have to pay our tax in cash. Taxation is merciless!

Perhaps only executives can appreciate this feeling. Employees may think it's just the company's money. But for us, it almost feels like someone is stealing our savings. That's why some executives will resort to any cheap trick to avoid paying taxes.

This, of course, is wrong. A company's profit does not belong to the executives. Further, the taxes we pay are used to benefit society. We should not selfishly hide our profit from taxation.

To avoid "tax resentment," we must look at our profit objectively for what it is. Profit is a grade or a score, like in a game, of the credit that society gives us in return for our contribution. When I look at profit that way, I can be more objective and not so possessive. In other words, only after-tax net profit is the true profit. Taxes are business expenses which we must incur. After-tax profit is the only profit given to us for our business efforts.

Think of taxes as necessary business expenses paid to support the communities in which we operate.

❧ Nourish Our Business ❧

Some owners of very profitable businesses deliberately take measures to keep their profit low. In other words, they splurge on lavish entertainment, boondoggle trips, and unnecessary expenses to reduce taxable income.

It is true that more than half of our profit is taken away each year in taxes. Still, the rest is left to the company. The true spirit of business management should be to cherish the after-tax profit.

It is said that the equity ratios of most Japanese companies are very low because of Japan's tax system. I rather think it is a matter of the philosophy of business executives.

Reinvesting the after-tax profit is the only way to nourish our business and make it stronger by creating a large internal reserve and a high equity ratio.

No matter how much we have to pay in taxes, we must never stop our efforts to raise our profitability.

I now treat taxes as a part of our necessary business expenses, and assiduously accumulate after-tax profits within our company.

Today, we have hefty internal reserves which provide stability and flexibility to our company and work opportunities for our employees. This strength also enables us to tackle challenging new ventures.

❧ Set a Visible Goal ❧

When we set our annual master plan, I challenge myself and others against setting low, easily attainable targets. Rather, I want each amoeba to have ambitious goals based upon our strong desire to achieve. I say, "Boast and then make it come true."

Even though someone may fail to achieve their plan, I do not necessarily go after the results only. But this does not mean it is all right to let our plans go unachieved; if the plan continues to be unachieved year after year, our employees will lose their confidence and ability to attain goals. It is important to meet our targets.

Everyone has to share the same goal to achieve a target. If the only people interested in attaining the goal were top executives, the goal would never be achieved.

Structure your company so that even the smallest units of the organization have their own plans. Entice each person to work hard to pursue his or her part of the plan and to help the division meet *its* plan. Then, as each amoeba's plan is met, the overall plan for the organization will be accomplished as a matter of course. Set plans every month to translate the annual plan into a more tangible and motivating target.

A master plan must be shared with all employees and translated into goals that are ardently desired by all.

ᴥ Wrestle in the Center of the Ring ᴥ

I always tell our people to wrestle in the center of the ring. That means to act on challenges immediately, and not wait until you are pushed to the edge of a deadline.

I am sure you have had the experience of studying through the night before an exam. Many of you must have run out of time and faced a test in a desperate mood. Since the time and date of an exam are scheduled beforehand, we should start sooner if we want to get a good grade. But many of us don't.

In Japanese Sumo wrestling, we see that some wrestlers wait until they are on the very edge of the ring and about to be thrown out before they really fight to defend themselves. I often wonder why they don't use their strength while they are still in the center.

Our business life is no different. When we are in the center of the ring, we feel relaxed because there is plenty of time and room to make our moves. Then we put forth a flurry of activity when we are pushed to the edge of the ring.

We should always pretend that there is no time or room left, and make our efforts long before we are actually about to be pushed out of the ring.

Prepare "reserves," then act as though you have no reserve at all. This is the secret of a stable business.

❧ Put Your Company Before Yourself ❧

Executives are often put in a position where they must choose between the company's benefit and their own. As executives, we should maintain a value system in which we automatically place our company's benefit first.

For example, there are two ways to list stock on a stock exchange. The company can offer stock which current shareholders own, or it can issue new shares for public offering.

The first method will bring premiums to the executives and other stockholders, perhaps even make them rich; but under the second method, the premiums go back into the company.

In my case, I decide without hesitation to issue new shares. That's because our employees are my partners, and they depend upon the company for their own and their families' future. It is most important that we enrich the company's equity position by accumulating the stocks' premiums, stabilizing the financial basis of the company, and giving assurance to our employees.

When faced with the choice of benefiting self or the group, it is the basic moral obligation of a leader—always and without any hesitation—to place the group's interest ahead of his or her own.

❧ The Bull and the Bear ❧

When a recession hits, many business owners look to government for a solution. They ask for additional spending, tax cuts, or lower interest rates to stimulate growth. Everyone seems to have his or her own opinion.

In truth, every economy has good and bad periods—and no single cycle has ever lasted forever. Japan, for example, has experienced many recessions of varying degree and used each one as a stepping stone to the next phase of growth.

On the whole, Japan's economy has progressed continually upward. But because of this historic background, many Japanese managers erroneously believe that their economy will keep growing forever.

The most fundamental fact about any economy is that it operates on a cycle. The bull and the bear are facts of life, and preparing for bad times during the good is the most basic rule of management.

Unfortunately, many of today's managers have forgotten this rule and have become weak-kneed—dependent on government or some divine intervention for a recovery.

In my opinion, the term "management" should refer to *managing*—building a reserve during good times so a recession won't leave us crying for help.

❧ The Bubble Economy ❧

The cycle of good and bad times is a matter of course in business. In fact, a painful recession teaches managers something precious: it instills within their hearts the desire to manage conservatively during the "boom," and to build a reserve that can outlast the inevitable "bust."

During Japan's so-called "bubble economy," however, anyone could get rich by simply buying land or stock. Debts of millions of dollars were nothing to worry about. Money came easily in vast amounts as if it simply bubbled up from nowhere. Yet nobody ever sounded a warning, and hardly anyone exercised restraint. Instead, an entire generation kept silent as the profits rolled in—and then, at the sight of the first loss, we panicked.

This mentality also led the stock market into a "loss-compensation" scandal. At that time, people were getting rich in stocks by simply entrusting large sums of money with securities firms. Once these people began to *lose* money, they had the nerve to demand compensation—and they got it!

Bulls and bears are the basic tenets of trading. Corporate financiers have attempted to defy this rule, almost as if they could defy gravity—and had they succeeded, they might have destroyed the entire stock market.

A Conversation with Kazuo Inamori on Profit

What is the secret of good business management?

We must understand that business management is, in the simplest possible terms, about increasing sales and reducing costs. There is nothing complicated about it. In business management, we must all try to maximize sales while minimizing costs. In doing so, we maximize our added value by turning low-value resources into high-added-value products and services that society appreciates. It is particularly important in a challenging economic climate to run a business according to the simplest formula—that is, optimizing profit by maximizing revenues and minimizing expenses.

Can you give us a practical example of "Wrestle in the Center of the Ring"?

To wrestle in the center of the ring means to have a reserve. If you want to grasp a business opportunity, you must be able to move swiftly. For that, you need to have saved your profit and have that reserve to act upon.

When we wanted to start DDI Corporation to compete against Nippon Telegraph and Telephone (NTT), we realized that we needed to spend at least 100 billion yen initially. No major corporation in Japan wanted to invest that kind of money. At that time, Kyocera had 150 billion yen on deposit in banks. When I discussed the idea of DDI to

Kyocera management, they said: "Even if you lost it all, we'd still have 50 billion yen in our deposits. That ought to be enough to keep Kyocera going."

That encouraged me to get started with DDI. Had we not had that kind of reserve, I would have had a very difficult time embarking on such a major project. This is what I mean by "wrestle in the center of the ring."

Should prices always be set by top management?

Once a pricing policy has been determined, the actual pricing may be handed off to a lower level of management. In other words, the pricing policy should be set at the top, but daily pricing responsibilities may be delegated.

Can't pricing mistakes be overcome through hard work?

We have all seen the case where a new discount outlet opens and customers flock to the store. Then, one day, we hear that the store has gone bankrupt. This is a case of a wrong "pricing policy," a management mistake. When the pricing policy is set incorrectly, no matter how hard we try, we may never be able to make the business a success.

Should products always be priced lower than the market price?

If your products are superior, they should be priced accordingly. If they are not competitive in quality or features, they have to be priced lower to make them worthwhile to the customers.

Otherwise, you may confuse your customers. The pricing should not be predatory or deceiving, but in harmony with the market, commanding the best price for the manufacturer and still at a level to create full customer satisfaction.

Wouldn't the amoeba system make each amoeba concerned only with its own profitability, or make each one self-centered and egotistic?

We don't just look at the P&L for individual amoebas, our smallest profit center units. For example, Kyocera has P&L for larger amoebas, like divisions and companies, which are made up of several amoebas, including the consolidated Kyocera worldwide.

Each department in an operating company lists its P&L in what we call the hourly efficiency (H/E) report which computes the "value added by the amoeba," and the "hourly efficiency" which is the added value divided by the total labor hours of all people in the amoeba. At the same time, a divisional H/E looks at the total picture for the division. Then the operating company has its H/E, and then a consolidated report is produced by world region. Finally, a global consolidated report is produced.

If one amoeba selfishly seeks to undermine another amoeba's interests, this will negatively affect the H/E of which this amoeba is only a small part. The executive in charge of the higher-level amoeba must intervene.

Is hourly efficiency measurement essential to amoeba management?

Not really. You could use the standard income statement at the amoeba level to keep track of your profit and loss. In fact, the hourly efficiency is compatible with the P&L statement. With P&L, however, it is more difficult to fairly compare two amoebas of different sizes. On the other hand, we can tell that an amoeba which has the hourly efficiency of $100 per person-hour is doing much better than one struggling at $10, regardless of where in the world they are operating or how many people each employs.

In the United States, dividing an organization into small units tends to raise indirect expenses. Wouldn't your hourly efficiency system for amoebas be too costly in the United States?

Not only in the United States, but even in Japan, most managers believe this. They say that keeping track of the profit and loss of each amoeba is too expensive. They say that it's too tedious to keep track of such minute details, and that keeping total figures is sufficient.

Obviously, if our hourly efficiency system took extra overhead, it would defeat its purpose.

But, even to get the total figures in any business, as they suggest, you still need to collect reports on how many units of each product are made. All it takes is for each operator to keep track of his or her daily activities, to write the records down and submit the data. At Kyocera, such data are recorded daily, and reports are produced on a monthly, if not weekly, basis. We basically have no extra overhead costs for running our hourly efficiency system.

What actions do you take when an amoeba's performance is unsatisfactory?

This depends on the circumstances.

If the weakness appears due to a lack of technology, we may transfer technology. If the leader is weak, we may send in a reinforcement. If the leader is not appropriate for the amoeba, we may change his or her assignment. We evaluate the amoeba's performance against the plan they have set themselves. They have the authority to run their business, but also the responsibility to meet their plans.

If you set your goals high, wouldn't that discourage employees?

What I am trying to say is what the American educator, Dr. William Smith Clark, once said when he helped establish Sapporo Agricultural College (now Hokkaido University) a century ago. Dr. Clark told his students: "Boys, be ambitious!"

Suppose that you are capable of reaching 100 percent, but you set your goal to be 90 percent, just to make sure you would attain it. Your conservatism will compound each time you set a new goal. On the other hand, if you were to set your goal above 100 percent and work hard to attain it, your next goal could be even more ambitious. This will lead to exponential growth.

Of course, you are right to say that setting unattainable goals is discouraging, especially to employees. Therefore, major goals must be broken down into attainable, incremental steps—with each step building more confidence and leading to a more ambitious future goal.

In 10, 20, or 30 years, there will be a big difference between people who have set incremental goals and attained them one at a time, those who have set unattainable goals and never reached them, and those who have never set any ambitious target.

AMBITION

*To succeed,
we must have a desire so strong
that it reaches and permeates
our subconscious minds.*

Ambition: Possess an Ardent Desire

- Nurture a desire so strong and so persistent that it becomes a part of your subconscious mind.

- An entrepreneur must first have a clear vision of how he or she wants the company managed. A mere dream of what you want is not adequate. Instead, cultivate a desire so strong and a vision so clear that they become a part of your subconscious mind. Such true ambitions should have specific and noble goals, causes, and ideals.

- Even with such strong desires, circumstances will change and affect management adversely. Still, do not use these circumstances as excuses. Your determination should be so strong as to overcome any obstacles, foreseen or unforeseen.

❧ Get Fired Up! ❧

There are three basic types of matter: combustible, noncombustible, and spontaneously combustible.

A combustible material starts burning when it is near a fire; a noncombustible does not burn, even when it is in the fire; and a spontaneously combustible material starts burning on its own.

I classify human beings in the same way. The most productive person is spontaneously combustible, a self-starter. That's because enthusiasm and passion are the basic factors necessary for achieving anything.

The noncombustible person is one who may be talented, but is nihilistic and insensitive, and cannot feel emotions. They are the people who have difficulty accomplishing anything worthwhile in spite of their abilities. Combustible people can at least become motivated when surrounded by motivated people. They can at least start burning when they are near the fire.

The kind of people we really need are spontaneously combustible, that is, those people who can become fired up with their own energy. Such people can burn and still give energy to others around them.

You must engulf others in your passion.

❧ Be the Center of Your Vortex ❧

There is a limit to what one person alone can achieve. In your work, you must cooperate with people around you—your supervisors, subordinates, and colleagues.

However, you should aggressively pursue your work so the people around you will spontaneously cooperate with you. This is what I call "working in the center of the vortex."

Unless you are careful, you might end up being outside the vortex with someone else in the center of it.

In a company there are many business vortexes, like currents eddying everywhere. If you are just floating around them, you will be engulfed in them.

To experience the real joy and zest of work, you have to be in the center of the vortex, and tackle your job as aggressively as if you were engulfing the other people around you.

Whether or not your way of thinking is independent and aggressive enough to create your own vortex will decide not only the result of your work, but also the result of your life.

❧ Never Stop Dreaming ❧

I call myself the "dreamer."

I habitually have the wildest dreams. I keep on dreaming boundless dreams one after another, and I develop my enterprises in the dreams.

I don't try to realize my dreams right away. I just keep dreaming and imagining intensely in my mind. I continue this simulation in my dreams day after day. We could refer to this process for building a strong desire as "passion."

Even when I am off work, I keep this desire in my mind.

When I walk down the street, something which is related to my desire will often jump into my sight and make a powerful impression. At a crowded party, for example, a person whom I desperately need to contact to make my dream come true may catch my attention from across the room.

If I didn't have a strong desire, these things and people would merely pass me by.

Wonderful chances are hiding among ordinary sights. But only the person who is strongly aware of his or her purpose can see them.

Vacant eyes without any goals will never be able to see the wonderful opportunities of life.

❧ Think You Can ❧

In the mid-'60s, I had an opportunity to hear a lecture by the late Mr. Konosuke Matsushita, one of the most highly revered businessmen in Japan. The title was "The Reservoir Method of Management."

He told the audience that we had to conduct business with a reserve, just as a water reservoir must always be kept filled with a certain amount of water.

During the question-and-answer session, a man in the audience praised Mr. Matsushita for the soundness of the concept—but indicated that he had no funds to spare. "How do I go about making the reserve?" he asked.

Matsushita replied that he as well did not know the answer. "Still," he continued, "you must believe that you need that reserve." The audience laughed but, personally, I was strongly impressed by that reply.

What I learned was that we must first think we can make it happen. If we keep telling ourselves "I know this would be ideal, but in reality, it is impossible," then nothing will happen.

We cannot strive for what we do not believe in.

If you have a strong desire, and truly believe that it will be realized, you will find a way out of difficult situations and achieve your goal.

❧ Is My Motive Virtuous? ❧

When I start a new business, there is one thing that I consider most important. I always ask myself, "Is my motive virtuous?" I want to make sure that the reason for starting the project is based on good intentions and not on a self-serving motive.

Zen, the Japanese word for "good," means being universally virtuous in anybody's eyes. I cannot achieve something worthwhile by considering only my own interests, my own convenience, or how I may appear to others. The motive has to be good for others as well as myself.

Once the project is under way, I continue to ask myself if the process is virtuous. If we dare to act wrongfully, we will eventually have to pay the price ourselves. In going through the process of implementing the project, we must not deviate from what is right as human beings.

In other words, we need to ask ourselves if our self-interest is not standing in the way of achieving our goal. An enterprise built upon a self-centered cause cannot earn its employees' trust or dedication.

If your motivation and methods are virtuous, you need not worry much about the result.

❧ Set a Higher Goal ❧

The goal we set as our business objective is very important. I believe that our objectives should represent our highest aspirations as human beings.

Why do we need a high objective? In order to survive in business, we must have passion and keep our energy level high. Our desire for money and fame promotes a guilty conscience and this can consume a lot of energy. Such a guilty conscience can lower our energy level for the task at hand.

As weak human beings, we need a cause to elevate us. We have an objective which other people, as well as our own conscience, will find unsurpassed. If we have an excellent objective that we can proudly tell everyone about, we can raise our energy level without fear or guilt. That is one reason that the objective of business should be to operate according to the highest moral standards.

The objective of business reflects the philosophy of the top executive. Frantic efforts can almost always produce temporary success, but if the CEO's philosophy is distorted, the business will be doomed to fail.

Only when we are successful in elevating our philosophy and view of life can we prevent ourselves from repeating the same mistakes—and losing the success that we have earned.

❧ Apply Your Gift ❧

When reflecting on the requirements of a leader, you might think you qualify because you have ability, the power to direct others, and a wonderful personality.

But there is something more you need to understand.

There is a reason you have been bestowed with such leadership talents. It was not inevitable that you had to have these talents. Someone else could have been born with them.

I think that each of us is born with specific talents in certain proportions. Some people are artistic, others are athletic; still others, may be given the charisma to guide groups of people to fulfillment.

Therefore, if you happen to have such talents, you should use them for the world, for society, and for the group, but never just for yourself. In other words, a person who was born with this gift of leadership has to fulfill his or her duties as a leader. You should never be arrogant or condescending just because you have been given this gift.

You should never monopolize your inherent talents. Rather, be humble and try to lead by using your talents for the group.

❧ Elevate Your Purpose ❧

There are various theories about the purpose of an enterprise. The target we set depends upon the company's overall purpose. We need to ask, "What kind of company do we want to be?"

For example, if your purpose is to become number one in your industry, you must prepare for the journey to reach that goal accordingly.

The factors that influence management have both visible and invisible components. The visible part is what we can physically account for, such as capital, R&D capability, machines, and equipment. The invisible part is the corporate culture, the philosophy and ideology expressed by management and employees.

All of these factors must function fully to achieve a higher goal. If we aim to be the top company in a given field, we are expected to have a top-notch company philosophy to match. This could demand a lot from both the employer and the employees. They would be expected to live according to very high standards.

When you say, "I want to make our company a world-class enterprise," or "I want to work for a great company," you must be willing to put in your share.

Corporate prestige does not come free.

A Conversation with Kazuo Inamori on Ambition

What do you mean by ambition?

First of all, a manager must set specific goals for the business. This means that you must have strong desires and visualize vividly in your mind what you would like yourself and your business to achieve. An excellent manager is someone who has a clear mental image of how the business should be run and who holds this image at all times. Having such an image only during meetings or only occasionally is not sufficient. A true ambition should stay with you 24 hours a day.

How can a motive be virtuous?

The Japanese word originally used was *zen*, meaning "good" as in a good deed, a virtue, or a charity. It's a very abstract term that originally came from Chinese, with a meaning that closely resembles the Christian ethic of "Do unto others as you would have them do unto you." I use it in that sense. First, find joy in making others happy, starting with people around you.

The opposite of *zen* is *aku*, or evil, which motivates people to act on their hatred, animosity, anger, jealousy, or other selfish motives.

In starting a venture, we need to ask the question: "Is it just for my own benefit, or does it benefit others, the community, and society?" To make a profit is not bad, per se. However, it is not virtuous if your making money depends on your partners, vendors, or customers losing money or similar benefits. If you cannot be sure that your venture is virtuous, at least make sure that it makes a profit without hurting anyone.

If leadership is a gift we are born with, does that mean that leaders cannot be trained?

A person may be a born leader, but most leaders are trained. In either case, it's a gift to have that ability. I have been teaching our people and conducting executive seminars because I believe that many excellent leaders can be developed through training.

Is there a difference between a dream and a vision?

I have been using the words "dream" and "vision" interchangeably. In the beginning we have a dream of wanting to accomplish something. It's an ideal. As we continue to pursue the same dream, it starts to become clearer, more detailed and colored. Now it is a vision. When I am in that state of mind, I know my vision can come true.

Can you give us an example?

I have had many such experiences. When I was doing research into types of ceramics, I often found myself completely lost, as if I were in a dense fog with no visibility at all. Still I kept thinking that the type of ceramics I was searching for had to be available. With all my heart, I kept believing, "I want to synthesize this kind of ceramic. It should have such and such characteristics. I know it's possible if I mix this and that and fire it in a furnace at such and such temperature until it becomes a cohesive mass." We call this "sintering."

In reality, when we mix ceramic ingredients and sinter, there are impurities and other factors that make the products different from what we envisioned. When I examined the results, I could see where I erred or where our control failed. My next vision would become more defined and more controlled. My life became a repetition of such pursuits, continuing to repeat experiments as I kept refining my dream.

It was my passion that kept me going.

Does this work outside of R&D?

My experiences have been the same in business. Passion makes us want to "get fired up" and "burn." Working in that condition I have learned to make success of many ventures.

When a series of failures occurs, it is easy to become discouraged. We want our passion to burn, but it's difficult to keep it fired up. If we don't like the job, we don't repeat it. Without practice, we cannot improve.

On the other hand, there are times when we become excited by jobs that we were not previously interested in but were forced into doing. When we start enjoying our job, we can practice and become better at it. Eventually, we can make it a success.

It's no different than learning to play tennis. You may not be good at playing tennis, but you like it. So, you continue to practice. As you continue to practice, your skill improves. One day, you may find yourself winning a championship.

In other words, we must make ourselves believe that we like our jobs. Then, as we repeat them, we become better and better. Soon, you become passionate, and success is virtually guaranteed.

SINCERITY

"You exist:
that's why I exist."
This outlook is the surest path
to harmony and peace.

Sincerity Begets Love and Harmony

- It takes two to have a business transaction, a buyer and a seller. A successful transaction is one in which both parties are happy—a win-win proposition. *Sincerity* is the foundation for such a relationship.

- Make your partner happy. There can be no long-term business success in which only one party benefits and others suffer. A successful manager must create harmony through sincerity and a deeply held *love* of other human beings.

- In business, even more than in athletics, a successful player must have a strong competitive mind. Deep down, however, the entrepreneur must also possess sincerity, compassion, and kindness. As a coach who demands the very best from every teammate, the leader must guide the team to victory in an honest and sincere manner. But unlike a sporting event, in which victory always produces a loser, a business victory should create *harmony*.

❧ Use Your Heart as the Base ❧

I have always strived to base my business on the human heart. More specifically, I have focused on ways of establishing and maintaining firm, trustworthy relationships with all of my people at work.

Just as a person has to love in order to *be* loved, we—top management—must be pure of heart in order to attract others of a similar nature and build bonding relationships.

That is why I try so hard as the head of our company to control my selfish instincts. I consciously strive to abandon self-interest to the extent that I could actually risk my life for the company my employees love.

While it may be said that there is nothing more fragile and mutable than the human mind, it is also true that *a bond of human minds* can be among the strongest of all known phenomena.

History is full of wonderful achievements brought about through the meeting of unselfish human minds. But history also contains abundant examples of depraved human minds leading to the destruction and unhappiness of large numbers of people.

Remember that your heart and mind attract others of a similar nature.

❧ Earn Customers' Respect ❧

Business is the continuing accumulation of trust; in fact, the more customers in whom we can instill a sense of trust, the more business we can expect.

The Japanese *kanji* character for profit (*mouke*) is a combination of two others: *shinjiru*, meaning "to trust" or "to believe," and *mono*, or "person." Trusting people—this is how *profit* has been said for centuries.

However, I believe there's more to it than that. Of course, trust is a necessity. We can gain trust by offering good products at low cost, on time, and with excellent service. But if merchants have high moral standards and personal integrity, they can do more than gain trust: They can earn the *respect* of their customers.

I believe that the secret of success is to earn our customers' respect. If our customers respect us, they will buy our merchandise unconditionally—even when a competitor offers a lower price.

Being virtuous means more than offering superior performance on price, quality, and delivery. It's a *philosophy* that business people should cultivate. In other words, it's the ability to make others spontaneously respect us. We cannot manage a great business unless we learn to acquire this quality.

Long-term business success comes from earning our customers' respect.

❧ Align Our Vectors ❧

We are born as individuals to live freely, and each of us naturally thinks differently. An ideal organization would be one in which harmony flourishes while each individual sincerely pursues his or her own initiatives, unfettered by instructions or demands.

Unfortunately, my experience tells me that this is only an ideal. In reality, an organization that cannot align its members often fails. If each individual follows a different intention, the group's collective energy will disperse and it will be unable to mount any concerted effort. Successful companies find a way to align these individual vectors in the corporate direction while encouraging personal initiative and development.

"Aligning our vectors" means agreeing on the same general value system. By sharing the most basic philosophy on why our company exists and how we can make it successful, we can coordinate our actions while providing each person with maximum freedom to develop his or her talents.

In a club or social group, fundamental disagreements can be a sign of vibrancy. But for an enterprise, an organization with a mission, it is essential that all members share the same basic values.

❧ Criteria for Decision Making ❧

Leaders must make decisions every day. To make good decisions, they must remain completely objective and unbiased. Scientists, for example, do not "eyeball" important measurements; they instead use a ruler, a micrometer, or some other standard. Similarly, leaders need a "ruler" or a standard if they wish to consistently make the right decisions.

Some people possess no such ruler. As a result, their decisions depend on the judgments of others, or on so-called common sense, precedence, or tradition.

Other people may have a self-centered ruler. Their standard of judgment is solely subjective, based on how advantageous a solution may be to them. Thus, their ruler is crooked. Still others have an accurate ruler but they exaggerate the reading because they are not sincere.

Life is an accumulation of decisions. If we can make wise decisions, we can live a wonderful life.

To make good decisions, you must have a sincere philosophy of life to use as your ruler.

Such a philosophy is formed by our own human reason and sense of fairness, righteousness, justice, kindness, thoughtfulness, harmony, and sincerity. We should use this philosophy as a ruler for our decisions and our lives.

❧ Be a Humble Leader ❧

A leader should always remain humble.

Power and authority tend to corrupt a person's morals and create arrogance and condescension. Under a leader who has qualities such as these, a team might attain temporary success, but it cannot continue growing for long. Eventually, team members will stop cooperating.

Unfortunately, society in general is becoming more self-centered—and our own standards of judgment can all too easily reflect this trend. Our general loss of humility produces needless, counterproductive confrontations.

On the other extreme is an old Japanese saying: "You exist: that's why I exist." We once acknowledged ourselves as a small part of the whole, and this remains the only way to maintain harmony and cooperation within a group. We should acknowledge that every fact has two aspects—and "see" from both sides.

To develop a sense of community, leaders must have the humility to recognize that they owe their positions to their subordinates!

Only a humble leader can build a cooperating team and lead it to harmonious, long-term success.

❧ Possess Dual Extremes ❧

An executive must have a balanced personality.

Business is a nonstop chain of critical decision making. Sometimes you must take a stand against the opposition of other executives, attorneys, or bankers. You still have to execute your plan with confidence and determination. Then, at other times, you may have to listen humbly to one of your employees, admit that you made a mistake, and courageously revise your plan.

In other words, you need both prudence and boldness. This does not mean you should be a neutral character who is neither prudent nor bold. An executive who has to make serious decisions must have more than just an agreeable personality.

The author, F. Scott Fitzgerald, once said, "The test of a first-rate intelligence is the ability to hold two opposed ideas in the mind at the same time, and still retain the ability to function."

As an executive you must occasionally reprimand an employee to the point of appearing heartless while hiding tears inside your heart.

A balanced executive is one whose single personality can possess dual extremes.

❧ Big Love, Little Love ❧

"You work late every day—even on Sundays and holidays. I feel sorry for your wife and family because you don't spend any time with them."

Many people tell me this...yet I don't believe I am sacrificing my family. My mission is not just to protect them or myself with a small love, but to make our employees happy with a great love.

I hesitate, however, to obligate anyone to have this love. You have to spontaneously awaken to it. If we force uninterested people into having this love, they would be caught in a dilemma between loyalty to their company and faithfulness to their family.

If they neglected their family and devoted themselves to their work despite this dilemma, they would not be true to themselves nor would they be successful on the job.

Still, I hope that others will indeed awaken to this great love and be willing to work for others, because I believe that only executives who are courageous enough to do so can bring happiness to their people.

A great love involves bringing happiness to a great number of people.

❧ Evaluate, Assign, Follow Up ❧

To train subordinates we must instruct them rigorously and clearly, assign them tasks, and promote their self-confidence. In other words, we must allow them to gain experience.

Before giving a subordinate an assignment, however, a leader must evaluate the employee's character. The leader must decide whether the employee is qualified to do the job in terms of both attitude and ability. In many cases, attitude is the more important criterion—since the attitude of the worker greatly influences the outcome of the work.

Once we find appropriate individuals, we can assign them specific tasks. Even then, I don't just leave everything to them. Every person has strong points and weak points. Therefore, I constantly observe and evaluate their performance.

I follow up on the progress of my subordinates by monitoring and supporting them in the areas in which they need help, or by placing someone else to assist them. At the same time, I coach them so they can learn to improve themselves on their own.

Leaders must have excellent personality traits and strong abilities. Without these, you cannot make a fair and accurate evaluation of your own subordinates.

❧ Guide with a Great Love ❧

A leader should treat his or her subordinates with love. By this, I do not mean affection. Rather, I mean managing through actions that display a "great love" instead of a "small love."

For example, one type of parent may spoil their children so much that they never have to achieve for themselves and thus become failures in life. On the other hand, children raised by more strict parents learn self-discipline and become successful. In the first case, the parent exhibits a small love; in the second, a great love.

At work, there are many kinds of managers. Some may be kind, listening to their subordinates' opinions and changing things to make life easier. Others may be strict.

If a manager is only trying to please subordinates without following any guiding principle, it will be detrimental to them and to the organization in the long run. Managers who are "easy" with subordinates may be more popular, but this laxity will spoil people. In the long run, subordinates will do better with strict managers who are willing to provide guidance, discipline, and training.

A great virtue may appear merciless, but small virtue is like a great vice. In dealing with subordinates, a leader who guides with a "small love" will achieve only temporary popularity and short-term success.

❧ Win Trust by Caring ❧

Executives in a fast-growing company must take the initiative to work aggressively and lead by example. We must be sincere in our intent—and most of all, as leaders, we must never forget to look back and make sure our employees are following.

Before employees will follow management, they must not only trust, but *respect* their managers. And the only way to establish such a bond is to work heart-to-heart on a daily basis.

If time does not permit us to remain in touch with each employee, we risk becoming the condescending, "sword-wielding" kind of executive. Thus, we must grasp and cherish every opportunity we have. Have a casual cup of coffee with your employees, or drop a relevant word of thanks for their hard work as you pass by.

These small, sincere considerations are sure to touch their hearts. And long-lasting relationships based on such consideration will foster community and harmony within the company.

Managing means giving both discipline and rewards when necessary. When employees see a warm heart beneath an executive's tough demeanor, they will be willing to follow.

&. Communicate with All Your Heart &.

Smooth talkers often play with words when they speak. They may be good orators and, on the surface, are easy to like. However, when you listen carefully, you will often find them as devoid of substance as cotton candy.

Some people mistake smooth talking for persuasiveness, but I don't find it appealing. In fact, I hesitate to speak with anyone who has such a frivolous personality.

My advice to young people is to avoid imitating these glib mannerisms. Instead, speak from your own heart, with words that come from the heart, no matter how faltering they may sound.

When you need to be understood, and you speak from your heart, your own words take on a special power—they reach into the hearts of others and evoke strong emotions. This is the highest form of persuasion, even when it lacks all eloquence and oratorical style.

If you want others to truly understand you, you must share your emotions. Do not practice the art of glibness. Instead, practice speaking sincerely with your whole body and soul.

Sincerity binds the listener to the speaker.

🐚 Bridge the Generation Gap 🐚

When you try to communicate your management philosophy to employees, you have to bridge the gaps in understanding that result from differences in age, lifestyle, and experience.

You may wish you were the same age as your employees so you would have more in common with them. Your lifestyles would be more similar, and you as manager could rely on common backgrounds to guide your employees into a better understanding of your views. But in reality, employees are usually more like your children—a generation removed. So the more you rely upon the traditions and values of your generation, the more difficult your philosophy will be for them to accept.

For young people to understand your philosophy, it must embody universal truths and principles that answer this question: "What is the right thing to do as a human being?" Then, even employees of different generations will come to embrace it.

Older people lament that the new generation takes the easy way and doesn't work hard. But we are all motivated by the desire to realize our dreams.

I believe that today's young people will take on incredibly challenging work if they can find their dreams in it. They *will* accept your philosophy if you can appeal to this common ground.

A Conversation with Kazuo Inamori on Sincerity

Why is sincerity a leadership quality?

Sincerity begets trust, trust begets respect, and respect enables you to lead your group. We often think of respect as something bestowed upon teachers or professors. It is rather unusual to think of respect as being essential to business executives. However, to bring your subordinates together, draw the very best from them, and develop their abilities, you must share a working relationship based on mutual trust. And this mutual trust cannot occur unless the leader is a considerate person who is sincere and cares about others.

Why do you say that we need to earn the respect of our customers, rather than their trust?

Obviously, respect and trust go hand in hand—but there is a difference. Trust is a basic prerequisite of doing business. Respect, on the other hand, is an elevated status that is much more difficult to earn.

When customers respect you, they are willing to listen to your opinions and suggestions. Instead of just giving you orders for their current needs, your customers will start to consult you about how best to design their new products. For example, if you are a components supplier, a customer who truly respects you may consult with you in the early design phases of their newest products. Your future business will be "designed in" because they respect your professional ability, commitment, and, above all, your personal integrity.

Can you give us an example of "small love"?

Thomas Watson, the founder of IBM, used to tell his people a story about an old man and wild geese. This old man lived by a lake where wild geese would stop every winter on their way to a warmer climate. One winter, a cold wave hit the lake and a few of the geese were trapped without food. The old man took pity on this small group of birds and started to feed them every day. Every winter thereafter, more and more geese would join them. Soon, the entire flock forgot about migrating and continued to enjoy the old man's hospitality all year long.

Then, one winter, the old man passed away. Without anyone to feed them, hundreds of geese starved to death.

The old man's kindness is an example of a "small love." A greater love might well have meant refraining from the temptation to help the small number of geese in the first place—and thereby save a much greater number of geese in the end.

Doesn't "big love" require sacrifices from your family?

Certainly, I would not be able to do what I am doing without my family's complete support. And I don't want you to think that it is a virtue to sacrifice your family for your business. It is not. However, being a top executive does mean carrying on responsibilities for your employees and for *their* families as well.

My children used to complain because the father next door would come home at five and play with his children every day. I, in contrast, worked late every night. A regular salaried worker can usually come home on time and look after his or her family's happiness. But an executive's family is often asked to sacrifice.

However, executives should explain to their children the reasons why they cannot spend as much time playing with them as other parents—in a quasi parental role, these executives are responsible for their employees and *their* families as well. They have to work hard so that these families do not have to worry about their day-to-day life.

It isn't be easy for small children to understand such a concept, but as they grow older they should begin to appreciate the "greater love" that their parents have possessed.

STRENGTH

*True strength lies
in having the courage
to do the right thing.*

Strength: Lead with Courage

- True strength has nothing to do with wealth, fame, or physical power. It is a matter of having the courage to do the right thing.

- Subordinates are very sensitive to any element of weakness on the part of their management. Leaders who act in unfairness or cowardice fail to create a sense of confidence throughout their work force.

❧ Have the Courage to Sacrifice ❧

Every leader must have the courage to willingly endure a personal sacrifice.

A tremendous amount of energy is required for a group to accomplish anything worthwhile. This energy comes at a high price, and the leader should be the first to pay it. Leaders can earn the trust of their subordinates only by showing the necessary courage to sacrifice themselves.

When we work together to improve our work environment, we must do so not for the convenience of the leader, but for the majority of the people who work there. The leader must set a good example by sacrificing all self-interest. Without the leader's courage, we could never reform or improve to any significant degree.

If leaders want the enterprise to benefit no one but themselves, subordinates will become similarly self-interested. They will not willingly follow their leaders. Only when a leader is willing to accept a personal sacrifice for the sake of others will subordinates' trust and respect grow. Then the subordinates will learn to give of themselves and work to attain harmony, order, and prosperity for the company.

Self-sacrifice is the price every leader should be willing to pay.

❧ Set a Moral Example ❧

Leaders must be courageous and righteous. They must not merely preach work ethics and the rules of the workplace—they are called to set a living moral example for every employee.

Leaders who act hypocritically will be forced to condone the wrongful acts of others, and this will cause confusion within the group. Subordinates will be unable to trust or respect their management, which will result in a lowering of the group's overall moral standards.

Effective leaders have the courage to adhere to the right course of action. If we make a mistake, we should bravely admit it, apologize to our team and subordinates, and move on. Above all, we must *never* quibble, attempt to shift the blame, or hide behind an excuse.

Our subordinates do, in fact, look up to us. We must be the first to demonstrate the example we want them to follow.

A leader's actions, behavior, and attitude—good or bad—will spread to other employees and engulf the entire team like a brush fire.

The team is a mirror that reflects its leader.

❧ Practice What You Preach ❧

In today's global business environment, executives have the grave responsibility of making globally correct decisions. But if executives don't have a healthy spirit of self-sacrifice, their decisions will all be self-serving.

The following is an example:

A certain Japanese executive is aware of the problem of trade friction, and recognizes that unless Japan redresses its trade surplus, it will be internationally isolated. This leader also agrees that Japan has to open its markets to imports. However, when it comes to his own industry, he keeps quiet or even opposes such liberalization.

Honne to tatemae is a Japanese expression meaning "what is said is not always what is intended!" A top executive can't have that attitude.

If top executives claim to be righteous but do not personally possess the courage to sacrifice, they will hesitate to make a correct decision that may prove unpopular or unfavorable to their own group. However, the making of "popular" decisions will eventually have negative consequences for their group and society.

The willingness to sacrifice is a test of every executive's human qualities.

❧ Open Your Own Future ❧

During an era of revolutionary change, such as the American Independence or Japan's Meiji Restoration, young people are called upon to shoulder new challenges with courage and confidence. History has been shaped by the ability of young people to carry out these reforms.

However, the privilege of carrying out such a mission will not be given to you automatically just because you are young. The leaders of the day thus ponder a difficult question: *What type of young person should be entrusted with shaping the future?*

In our workplace, we look for those who possess insight and a certain eagerness to voice their opinions. We seek those who are full of ambition and willing to give their superiors continual suggestions. These are the ones who will improve the workplace and the enterprise for which they work.

Youths of this type must not only study hard, but also exhibit a clear and honest heart. They must demonstrate a spirit of self-sacrifice as well, since nobody will listen to self-serving ideas.

The most important traits of all are strength, courage, and willpower.

Unless you have the courage to risk your own career for a noble cause, you will never influence other people significantly or carry out a great reform.

❧ Prepare for a Challenge ❧

Challenge and *innovation* are popular, pleasant-sounding words. In reality, however, they lead to hardships and risks that require unimaginable amounts of hard work, patience, and courage.

In my opinion, we should not even say the word *challenge* until we have gathered the necessary ingredients for innovation. We must be able to back this word up with the courage to face a challenge and the stamina to withstand long, crushing hardships.

In Japan, a person who uses the word *challenge* without preparing any such backup is called a *banyuu,* or a reckless fool.

Only if we are well prepared mentally can we continually challenge ourselves to innovate in business management. Additionally, our enterprise must be in good financial shape, with enough capital to launch new projects and sail them safely to completion. When you want to innovate, you must begin with a firm conviction, extreme courage, daily perseverance, and the skills acquired through personal experience.

Extensive financial and mental preparation is necessary before we can challenge and innovate.

❧ Be Tough on Yourself ❧

In the words of an old nautical saying, "a sailor has only one plank between him and his death."

Employees of a new venture company are in a similar situation. However, as the venture grows and becomes successful, a greater number of young people will take the company's affluence for granted. The employees' attitudes and enthusiasm change.

This is understandable. You can't ask passengers aboard a luxury liner to act like boat people on a fishing raft—people with "just one plank" between them and a watery grave. They would not take you seriously.

When we started our company, we had no choice but to work with a real sense of crisis. Now that we have good facilities and abundant capital, however, it is spiritually more difficult to start a new venture with the same *kiki-kan*, or spirit of urgency. Unfortunately, without this spirit, we never could have gotten where we are today!

We must cultivate our spiritual strength and willpower to continually challenge our own limitations. Only the master of oneself can accept personal hardship and be earnestly dedicated to the success of a business.

You must have the strength and courage to drive yourself to the limit if you are to open new and challenging paths in today's affluent world.

❧ Devote Yourself to Business ❧

A true manager is a person who can lead a business wholeheartedly, with intense intellect and strength.

Understanding management techniques and management theory, no matter how important these may be, won't make a person an effective business executive.

The *true measure* of a top manager lies in how long he or she has worked in that capacity, totally devoted, spending every day with a tremendous sense of responsibility and self-sacrifice.

It is utterly arduous to totally devote oneself to business. To really do so, you will probably have no time left for yourself, and the responsibility may be mentally and physically unbearable. However, you will not be able to attein the qualities of a real chief executive unless you experience and overcome these hardships.

There is a world of difference between someone who works as a top executive and someone who does not.

Some want to leave all the decisions to the boss, because they view themselves as mere employees. Others are willing to risk their lives to make their business succeed.

A Conversation with Kazuo Inamori on Strength

What do you mean by strength?

By strength, I mean that a manager must have courage. A leader cannot act cowardly. In a tough, highly competitive business environment, employees, customers, and shareholders all have high expectations of you.

A cowardly manager can easily be tempted to make things look better than they actually are—perhaps by exaggerating sales figures by not including losses from returned goods, or by inflating profit figures by accumulating insufficient reserves for bad debts.

The manager's subconscious fear of criticism can lead to hiding the true status of the company. This should never happen. Especially in times of difficulty, employees need a strong, decisive manager who both exhibits and inspires courage.

What is the source of your strength?

In my case, I find strength in holding deep personal convictions. I believe others do as well. Incredible strength is often required to do the right thing. If there is even a hint of a misgiving or reluctance, confidence is shaken and courage is lost.

I was once told that 99 percent of all physicians refuse to diagnose and treat their own loved ones in the event of a serious illness, especially one requiring surgery.

Many reasons have been cited to explain this. Perhaps surgeons fear that their hands may hesitate or that their own emotions may make them too unsteady to perform a delicate operation on a loved one. Their feelings get in their way, and they would rather trust the skill of a colleague than their own. But that should not be so. If you had true courage and confidence in your skill as a physician, you might not turn your loved ones to your colleagues, but perform the very best operation yourself.

One key to strength is to have the courage to remain completely objective. Another is to believe in your ability with a conviction that goes deeper than your own emotions.

Can you give us examples of how leaders sacrifice their own convenience for the benefit of the work force?

I have seen some top executives locate their company headquarters at a remote location, far from their plant or sales operations, for the sole reason that it is most convenient to themselves. On the other hand, I know of one international company where executives do not have "preferred" parking spots reserved for themselves. Their belief is that they are there to serve their employees and customers, not to take advantage of them.

How have you or your own managers sacrificed personal gain for the sake of your employees?

Any sacrifice we make should come from the heart.

For example, when the recent renovation project started at the San Diego plant of Kyocera America, Inc., management there decided to start with areas that affect our employees the most. As a result, the production areas, training rooms, cafeterias, and washrooms have all been upgraded and remodeled. They will renovate the executive offices last, if at all.

Perhaps more significantly, when Kyocera had its first public stock offering, executives decided against selling our own stocks. Doing so could have made us wealthy overnight. Instead, new shares were issued, so that all the money that was raised flowed directly into the company to strengthen its financial position. In fact, rather than cashing in shares we owned, we in senior management created a stronger company for all employees.

On a personal level, I learned of a real estate project several years ago that was intended to renovate the downtown area of a North American city. The local Kyocera management was willing to invest in the project, but I considered it risky. I could not bear to see the company risk money on it, so I offered to make the investment myself—not out of speculation, but because it was a good project for the community.

As a result, the tallest building in that city was built and new shopping areas and condominiums sprouted up around our project. My original concerns were justified, however; I lost every dollar I invested in that project, but at least no Kyocera money was sacrificed.

Isn't being popular important for the leaders who want to keep peace in their group?

When Kyocera decided to establish world regional headquarters, I told the presidents of the regional management companies that they must be prepared to be unpopular. By this, I meant that, just as parents must practice "tough love" with their children, the exercise of "great love" will often make them unpopular. Being popular is a luxury that cannot be afforded when we are constantly subjected to the new challenges of a changing global environment. We must have *kiki-kan,* or a sense of urgency.

But being popular and creating harmony have nothing to do with each other. A popular politician can drive a nation into war.

INNOVATION

*What we like to do next
is what people tell us
we can never do.*

Innovate Constantly

- To innovate, always do your work better than you did yesterday. Tomorrow, do things one step better than you did today. Think creatively to improve your job regardless of how trivial it may seem.

- Major technological developments do not begin merely from a sophisticated technology or earth-shaking discovery. Constant efforts to improve current technology, over time, accumulate into a major gain.

- Try to get everyone involved in the improvement process through creativity. Even a simple task like cleaning the workplace can be improved through creative thinking and experimentation. A logical mind, creative thinking, and continuous experimentation are the foundation of any science.

- Make innovation a lifelong habit.

❧ Leaders, Be Creative ❧

Leaders must always have a creative frame of mind—and they should cultivate among their employees the desire to constantly seek and create something new.

Unless a leader continually introduces something creative into the group, it cannot be expected to continue to make progress and develop. If leaders are content with things as they are, they will influence the group to be satisfied with the status quo. This will lead to regression. If your leader is that kind of person, it's a tragedy for your group.

Creativity can arise only from the deep, difficult process of focusing both our conscious and subconscious minds. It is not born from shallow, impulsive thinking, or from halfhearted thoughts. Don't hope for spontaneous inspirations of creativity unless you have been preparing for them deep within your mind.

The creative spirit pursues a lasting desire.

Leaders must be able to create from their own profound thinking, suffering, and agonized efforts in the quest to achieve a goal.

❧ Simplify Your Thinking ❧

Managers continually face many different problems, and by the time top management hears about them, they have usually become greatly complicated.

Top managers are asked to analyze each problem and create a solution. However, the problem has usually become so tangled that one clear answer is all but impossible to find.

We can almost never solve a problem the way it is presented to us. Instead, like untangling a thread, we must find the beginning and try to determine how it became tangled. We trace the problem back one step at a time until we can understand how and why it became so complicated.

Often, the situation that led to the problem is surprisingly simple—and from there, we can see the solution. Yet many people attack a tangled problem in the tangled state, tugging at loose strings and tightening the "knot" until it becomes virtually impossible to solve.

People tend to complicate simple situations.

In management, as in R&D, we must develop the ability to extract the essence from a multitude of phenomena.

❧ Burst with Energy ❧

Unless we actively challenge ourselves in new fields, the future will be bleak for business and society in general.

Whether we are talking about technological development or marketing, challenging ourselves in new fields is always a difficult task. Obstacles we have never experienced before await us. We may fall into hardships we have never even imagined, and tremendous energy will be required to pull us out.

I tell people that you have to be somewhat fanatical in order to accomplish anything really worthwhile. Your passion must be all-consuming.

Passion is the energy of a person who knowingly attempts to overcome a seemingly insurmountable barrier. Fiery zeal, tremendous willpower, determination, and tenacity are all sources of energy for breaking through a barrier. This energy is the necessary factor in overcoming any challenge, and being a bit fanatical is the state in which you are filled with this tremendous energy.

To overcome new challenges, we must amass our energy into an outburst of human potential that will propel us toward success.

❧ Raise Your Mental Dimension ❧

Dr. Heisuke Hironaka is a world-renowned mathematician who found ways to solve difficult problems easily by raising the dimension of an equation. A complex phenomenon, he says, is merely the projection of a simple fact.

To comprehend this, imagine a traffic intersection without a signal. If many cars enter from all four directions, there is sure to be a pileup.

Now, if you add another dimension and give the crossing multiple levels, the cars can continue without even slowing down. If you are high above the crossing looking down, you may see only a flat, two-dimensional view. Cars approach at full speed and meet at the intersection, but instead of crashing, they appear to go through each other intact.

Life and society often seem hopelessly complicated. They involve relationships with colleagues, relatives, and friends, and we are often overwhelmed by the sheer complexity of it all. But this aspect of life is also a mere projection of a simple fact—and that fact is our own mind. In business, as in science, we often agonize over the puzzling complexity of a phenomenon by simply failing to rise and see it from a higher dimension.

To solve any complex problem, we should first elevate our minds and view the situation from a higher dimension.

❧ Face Difficulties Head-On ❧

An innovator is a pioneer who is willing to face any difficulty with humility and faith.

Do not avoid facing a difficult situation when you have a problem to solve. Instead, face the situation head-on.

To do this, your mental state must be charged with a certain tension. You must be determined to accomplish your goal at any cost; yet at the same time, it is important not to let preconceptions blur your view. You have to look at all aspects of the situation with open eyes—if you have any subjective bias or self-interest, the truth will evade you.

Finally, even though you may feel an urgent need to solve the problem immediately, you must keep an honest and humble attitude to review the situation in minute detail. If you remain truly humble, you may suddenly find what you have overlooked. I call this revelation "a whisper from Heaven."

Only when you are humble, sincere, and virtually begging for Divine intervention, can you obtain a really creative inspiration. For that, however, you must first be willing to face your difficulties head-on.

🐦 Don't Lose Your "Base" 🐦

Mountain climbers face the ever-present risk that a fog may descend in the middle of an expedition and reduce visibility to zero. Rather than getting completely lost, however, experienced climbers simply return to their "base camp" and start over.

I believe that this strategy also applies to building a new business or starting a difficult research project.

In a new venture, you will run into blank walls and experience gridlock time after time. You will be preoccupied with urgent distractions. And even when you manage to overcome them, you may find they have actually created a gap between your goal and reality. After overcoming so many immediate obstacles, you may find yourself further removed from your original destination.

You may congratulate yourself and be pleased with your conquests. But the result is far from success.

This situation occurs when you make tentative decisions without returning to your "base camp"— your principles and truths.

A decision based upon the essence of a matter will bring you success even in an unexplored area.

🐦 Reach for True Creativity 🐦

The late Dr. Michitaro Tanaka, Professor Emeritus of Kyoto University, once said, "The process of invention and discovery is the domain of *philosophy*. Only when the concept is logically proven does it become *science*." I was deeply impressed.

Tanaka believes that there is a big gap between common knowledge—which has already been scientifically explained—and true creativity. Inventions and discoveries are mental activities that bridge this gap. No amount of scientific common knowledge can produce true creativity.

Galileo Galilei advanced the theory that the sun is the center of the universe (heliocentrism). In his time, however, the *earth* was thought to be the center of the universe (geocentrism), and his work was suppressed because it was only a philosophical concept. But Galileo remained firm in his belief. Later, heliocentrism was proved and eventually accepted as science.

The way to true creativity is not through the accumulation of existing scientific knowledge. It starts with a leap of inspiration. This inspiration forms a philosophy and when it is proved and accepted, it finally *becomes* science.

True creativity blooms when we dare to reject "common sense" and traditionally accepted scientific knowledge.

❧ Rely on Yourself ❧

When I embark on a new project, I consider it most important that I move straight ahead along my chosen path. I avoid compromise, even when I encounter unexpected predicaments.

In a way, this behavior almost describes that of a rebel, a free spirit.

A rebel may resist his parents, defy the establishment, turn his back on authority, and try to have his own way.

But the real characteristic of a rebel is independence. A rebel does not compromise with the majority or pretend to understand others. Being independent means being free. A rebel does not depend on anyone else.

By relying solely on oneself, a rebel can be truly creative. By removing all hindrance, a rebel can pursue his or her own strong beliefs. Creativity cannot be born without that freedom.

No matter what field of innovation you pursue— business, science, or art—you cannot be truly successful without this spirit of freedom and rebellion against tradition.

🌿 Japanese Management 🌿

Japanese management once attracted global attention. It was very difficult for Westerners to understand why employees work so hard for a company. Many observers concluded that Japan must have had some magical management system.

But they were wrong. The Japanese work force has been rooted in a tradition that values diligence. The reason some Japanese enterprises excel is that their employees share this set of values and work hard for the company.

In the next decade the new generation, which grew up in more affluent times, will form the majority in the work force, and individualism will come to the forefront. The decline of Japanese companies could thus begin if excessive individualism leads their people to lose appreciation for the value of work.

In the United States today, companies like Hewlett-Packard and Motorola, which advocate corporate ideals and philosophy, continue to prosper. No company should rely solely on employees' native diligence or traditional values to succeed. We must set forth a company philosophy for our young employees, share with them the real meaning of work, and give them a purpose in life.

Japan, Inc. has no magic management system. There is simply no substitute for a conscientious work force.

A Conversation with Kazuo Inamori on Innovation

You preach innovation like an evangelist. But what happens within a start-up or small-scale company where you don't have the luxury of a big R&D budget?

This is when innovation becomes absolutely critical.

Can you give an example of how to go about it?

Kyoto Ceramic, Ltd., as Kyocera was originally named, was founded in 1959. Its core was what is now called our Fine Ceramics Group.

From the beginning, this group has always adopted unique ideas. We explored new applications in semiconductors, fishing rods, ceramic knives, and virtually any promising area. The most successful of our applications is the ceramic package for integrated circuits. At that time, making high-quality ceramic packages by sandwiching electrodes between thin ceramic sheets, and then laminating and sintering them, was a completely novel idea. Experts told us we could not do it. By 1994, however, our yearly sales of semiconductor packages had reached $1 billion.

Later, I came up with the idea of developing a ceramic heater expanding on the same laminating technology employed for semiconductor packages. Today, Kyocera's ceramic heaters are accepted worldwide as original and unique products in automobiles and other applications worth over $50 million in fiscal year 1994.

As the head of a company, how would you promote innovation?

First, I ask everybody to make today better than yesterday, then make tomorrow better than today. This is what we call *kaizen*.

Second, as the head of the enterprise, I must lead the way by personally being creative and encouraging others to follow.

Third, I pay special attention to make sure such efforts continue every day, incessantly, 365 days a year.

Finally, I avoid looking for a magical "quick fix" that will make the company grow. Instead, I try to rely on daily innovative efforts to develop the enterprise naturally.

You say it's important to have a clear vision. How do you go about creating a clear vision when innovation takes you "where no one has gone before?"

I personally try to concentrate on a goal so intently that it becomes programmed into my subconscious mind, which can model and simulate. Anyone with a sufficiently strong desire can do the same.

What is important is to continue working on our dream regardless of what we now lack. When we started Kyocera, we spent months planning, dreaming, reflecting, and arguing. When we started DDI

Corporation, we did the same. Today, DDI is considered the most successful challenger to the former monopoly held by Nippon Telegraph and Telephone (NTT).

We started DDI with five extremely competent young engineers from NTT. Every weekend, these five engineers would travel from Tokyo to Kyoto. We spent the weekends at Kyocera's guest house, *Warin-an,* discussing how to build DDI and make it a success. We continued this every weekend for six months, until our vision started to become clear.

Only after our vision had become so clear that we were convinced of its viability did I decide to go ahead. We faced many obstacles, but our clear vision always found a way around them. We had no real anxiety. Rather, we had confidence that our dream would come true. Ten years later, as of March 31, 1994, DDI has reached consolidated annual sales of almost $3.8 billion, with a pretax profit of $507 million.

OPTIMISM

Conceive optimistically;
plan pessimistically;
and execute optimistically.

Optimism: Always Remain Positive

- Always be cheerful, positive, and full of enthusiasm even in the most trying situations. Remain open-minded and excited about your goals at all times. Banish any sense of doubt or negativity from your mind.

- Realize that being an entrepreneur requires relentless determination, effort, and a willingness to face countless risks. Do not allow these challenges to make you negative, pessimistic, or cynical in your views.

- Remind yourself daily that a cheerful disposition invites success. It is difficult for any nihilist, cynic, or pessimist to become successful in a positive endeavor. But more important, the attitude of the leader—positive or negative—will directly influence the work force and how they deal with customers, suppliers, and each other.

❧ Begin with a Vision ❧

I never have any real doubts or anxieties when I start a new venture.

That doesn't mean I expect smooth sailing; in fact, I anticipate major obstacles every step of the way. Still, I don't have a bit of anxiety.

The reason is that I never start a project until I can clearly visualize its successful completion and the pathway that leads to it.

Success requires us to mentally visualize every potential obstacle and detour to reach our goal no matter what. Even if the project has never been attempted before, it must be familiar enough to create a sense of "déjà vu" when we begin.

To reach that point, we have to concentrate intensely on the project day in and day out. We imagine every contingency until no unforeseen problem remains. We perform this mental simulation repeatedly until a clear visual image starts appearing in our minds. I continue this until the vision takes on vivid, brilliant colors.

A clear vision produces tremendous confidence, fortifies your will to work hard, motivates others, and leads them to success.

❧ Get High on Your Dream ❧

To make your business successful, you must first have a dream that you can get "high" on.

Ironically, we are often cautioned *against* becoming intoxicated by our dreams, because business requires serious financial analysis and conservative planning. People who warn us against getting high on our own goals fear this will make us reckless and imprudent.

Nonetheless, I believe that a deep passion is needed to start any business and make it successful without giving up in the face of difficulty.

For example, I would never have been able to start DDI had I not been intoxicated with the dream of challenging the national monopoly of NTT. The project required a huge investment and nobody could guarantee our success. Any traditional mind would have judged the venture too risky.

Becoming intoxicated with a dream gives us the passion to bring it into reality.

Of course, one must become "sober" as soon as the project starts. Having committed ourselves, we must rely on logic to avoid undue risk, create a practical action plan, and bring the project to its successful completion.

🐦 Remove Any Fear of Failure 🐦

An American journalist once asked me why our company has been so successful. I thought for a while and said, "It's probably because we never punish an employee for failing." She looked puzzled, so I had to explain.

If one of our employees should fail during the course of earnestly pursuing a challenge for the sake of the company—and even cause considerable damage to the company—no punishment of any kind is meted out. If the challenge was taken on for the sake of our company and its employees, and if the employee's efforts were sincere and unselfish, there is no reason for punishment.

Sometimes we actually surprise an employee who has failed on a project by giving him or her another assignment right away. Though the previous project failed, the employee may have earnestly learned enough from it to move on.

Our corporate motto is "Respect the Divine and Love People," and this offers each employee the opportunity to do his or her best without any fear of failure—as long as it is done for the right cause and with a sincere heart.

Allowing the freedom to fail has given our employees the courage to continuously take on new challenges and try even harder.

❧ Manufacturing Is an Art ❧

If you look at any production floor, you will see some operators who have rhythm in their work and others who do not. Some operators move smoothly, gracefully, and effortlessly as they produce; each step flows into the next with no wasted motion. It is a real pleasure to watch them work.

Then there are others whose motions appear sluggish and artificial. Each step is an abrupt stop-and-go motion, often interrupted by unnecessary repositioning. It almost pains one to watch them.

If you were to compare their productivity, you would find that the graceful operator produces more parts, maintains a higher yield, and remains energetic.

As an analogy, consider the game of golf. The world's best players have their own distinct stances and swings. But one glance at any of them in action will capture our admiration and even inspire awe. The same can be said of sports other than golf—and indeed, even of our work.

If we always strive to be productive and efficient—and to make products of the highest quality—our motions will attain a captivating degree of beauty.

Just as an object of art reflects the passion of the artist, a production line reflects the passion of the operators and the management that inspired them.

❧ Break Free of Common Sense ❧

Some companies constantly show a five percent profit, even when the economy changes drastically.

This is because the top management itself believes five percent to be an average profit rate. They have a strong subconscious preconception which keeps their profit at five percent. When profit starts to drop, their subconscious minds make them take action so the five percent rate is maintained.

Of course, their profit never exceeds five percent, either. This is the fearsome power of the mind. Although it maintains the status quo, in this case, it also rules out drastic improvement. Some managers never raise their profit rate to 10 percent or 15 percent merely because they subconsciously believe five percent to be their limit.

These people have set up their goals according to "common sense." When they achieve their expected profit rate, they are satisfied with the result; they stop expecting any further improvement.

We should not run any business based on preconceptions. Unless we are "mentally free," how can we think creatively and expect record profits?

A leader must break away from the bonds of "common sense."

❧ Develop a Positive Outlook ❧

Before we can make any correct decision, we must first be able to assess the situation clearly. However, this is easier said than done.

While there can be only one fact, every phenomenon is perceived according to the observer's viewpoint. Because the phenomenon is viewed through the filter of the observer's mind, the same fact may be interpreted as either good or bad. This is our daily experience.

Facts are "filtered" through our hearts.

Take, for example, a man who labors intensely. You may see him as a sincere person trying to live his one life on earth as earnestly as he can. In this case, his work is a virtue.

But you may also see the same person as a workaholic who labors frantically with no regard for his health or family, and who knows no enjoyment. Now his work is a vice.

I am not saying which is correct; life is not so black and white. But if we are uncertain, we should trust in the goodness of others and think positively.

Negative thoughts will not help us grow or solve problems. Perceptions and judgments based on a positive mind are more likely to bring success.

❧ Conceive Optimistically ❧

Conceive optimistically, plan pessimistically, and execute optimistically.

In developing a new product, technology, or business, those who can conceive optimistically are most likely to succeed.

The most important factor in starting any new project is having a dream and the passion to achieve it. In setting your vision, you need to be ultraoptimistic. You must first believe that you have unlimited potential. Continue telling yourself, "I can do it," and believe in yourself.

Once you begin making your plan, however, you must become a pessimist. You should review your concept conservatively. By this I mean that you must recognize every potential difficulty, believe in Murphy's Law, and plan for all contingencies.

Equipped with such an ultraconservative plan, you should then move to execute it optimistically. Pessimism at this stage would prevent you from taking the bold action necessary to succeed.

It is essential that you master the ability to switch your viewpoint in this manner, from optimism to pessimism, and again to optimism.

A Conversation with Kazuo Inamori on Optimism

How can a leader remain optimistic during hard times?

A leader must always be cheerful and positive—*especially* in the gloom of a recession. The way to do this is to remain convinced of the viability of your own vision and to share this conviction with your subordinates. In difficult times, it is especially important to see reality as it is and to devise strategies that are best suited to the situation at hand. Remember that the economy runs in cycles, and therefore, an optimistic leader—someone who expects a recession to turn around—can lead the group toward a more positive direction than a pessimist who expects things to grow continually worse.

Does your concept of optimism apply to daily life?

Let me cite an author who has impressed me very much. In his book, *Success Is Never Ending, Failure Is Never Final*, Robert H. Schuller says that having a positive outlook on life is *the most important prerequisite* to having a successful life as a human being. I agree completely. It's important to believe that the outcome of your life will be exactly what you expect it to be. Why not start out by expecting a very positive result?

How does Kyocera actually practice your advice to "conceive optimistically, plan pessimistically, and execute optimistically?"

To conceive optimistically, at Kyocera, we often use *compas* where managers and employees meet in an informal atmosphere after hours. The name *compa* comes from the word *companions,* and it implies a time for fellowship and enjoyment. But it is also the place for education, frank discussion, brainstorming, and sharing dreams.

I regularly use a *compa* to discuss new ideas and paint outrageous dreams, trying to get people excited. One outrageous idea invites others, and soon everybody becomes excited about a project. An abundance of outrageous ideas is conceived in this "ultraoptimistic" fashion. Yet, out of such outrageous ideas come some very worthwhile and practical visions. Many projects are first conceived in this very optimistic manner.

Once we have decided to embark on a new project, we require that a detailed and conservative plan be formulated, building in all safeguards and contingencies. After much groundwork the plan is put on paper, and an executive approval document known as a *ringi* is prepared. This document is reviewed from all angles, then routed through internal approvers who scrutinize it and add their own comments, ending up on the desk of the final decision maker. Important *ringis* are reviewed by the board of directors. In short, *ringis* are used to prevent potential problems and business mistakes.

Each *ringi* is initiated by one individual who is responsible for the plan. It reflects the capability, efforts, and above all, the passion that the initiator has for the project. The business plan must be sound and worthy of the company's precious resources.

But, no matter how good a plan is, we never approve a *ringi* unless a capable person is assigned to carry it through responsibly and successfully.

Once a *ringi* is approved, it is incorporated into our yearly master plans and monthly plans. We ask people to be optimistic and bold, and yet responsible. I tell them to "boast and then make it come true." Any financial projections the plan may contain are not the same as the more conservative estimates that we publish and give externally to our investors. Instead, our plan represents ambitious execution targets that really challenge our limits.

At management meetings in which each group presents its master plan, leaders may be criticized for lacking ambition almost as much as for lacking realism. Each amoeba tries to remain optimistic as it does all it can to meet the master plan, a target it sets for itself and a plan upon which other amoebas' plans depend.

How did the compa *come to Kyocera?*

It originated at Kyocera when I used to meet with employees that I needed to win over. I tried to share my vision, my enthusiasm, and make them understand how this vision could benefit all of us. Often I got carried away in our discussions and forgot time. So I offered to have a meal or a drink, or even sing songs together and share our ideas informally. I wanted to use every opportunity to communicate, motivate, and get to know my people. As the company grew, I continued to use this format to motivate my colleagues and fellow employees, and the name *compa* was given to it.

NEVER GIVE UP

If you have a strong desire,
and truly believe that
it will be realized someday,
you will find a way out
of impossible situations
and achieve your goal.

Never Give Up: Try Harder than Anyone Else

- Success lies in a person's willingness to make relentless, step-by-step efforts, even on mundane tasks. This may sound simplistic, but the person who continues working more earnestly than anyone else will always achieve success.

- Aim at a goal that is so far away it makes you wonder whether your "daily steps" make any difference at all—but let those steps accumulate!

- Remember that even the greatest accomplishments are nothing more than the accumulation of small, seemingly trivial tasks. There are no valid shortcuts to long-term success.

- Keep one firm conviction in your heart at all times: *You have not failed until you stop trying.*

﴾ Elevate Your Desire ﴿

Elevate your desire until it becomes a conviction.

I don't think any of us should be a slave to circumstance. Some people seek a goal but give up easily, thinking that social conditions or economic factors make their goal impossible to realize. The more they study and understand their circumstances, the more convinced they become that their dream is unattainable.

If only they would cling to their dream with an intense desire, they could continuously devise better ways to make it come true. If you desire something from the bottom of your heart, your mind will work to overcome every obstacle in your path—even as you sleep. That is precisely how incredible efforts and true creativity are generated.

A slave to circumstance will only understand the unfortunate nature of a situation and conclude that the dream was unrealistic. But a person with a strong desire will start devising ways to solve the problem and not give up until the goal is reached.

The intensity of our desires is the biggest difference between those of us who move forward purposefully, those who keep stumbling, and those who idle their lives away.

❧ Pursue Your Infinite Possibilities ❧

"Where can I find a good idea?"—We tend to look outside our own minds for inspiration.

I first look *inside*. After pursuing all the possibilities of a specific task, striving to improve and manage it, I often discover a great innovation I had never even imagined.

Some people, unaware of how I accomplish such feats, see the result and remark that I must have the gift of clairvoyance. Of course, I have no such gift.

But if you insist that I do, then each of you can surely acquire the same ability by pursuing enthusiastically every opportunity for improvement you can find. I would rather call this *foresight*, not *clairvoyance*.

In order to survive in an era of uncertainty, it is very important to acquire this foresight—but we cannot obtain it from the outside world. We have to develop it within ourselves by pursuing every possibility around us, taking full advantage of our technology and experience.

No matter how much times change, the only golden road to innovation is to carefully examine what we already have and pursue further possibilities.

🐦 Be a Stern Taskmaster 🐦

I have high expectations of my employees. They accept my challenges because we do not have a hereditary system within our company. If we were a family business, my employees might think my demands came from selfish greed for my family.

The reason I am against the hereditary system is that the second generation may not be able to inherit and pass on the original management philosophy of a particular enterprise.

Philosophy is what creates a corporate identity, and the enterprise cannot continue its path to prosperity without maintaining this philosophy.

I want to entrust the future of our company to employees who possess wonderful personalities, abundant passion, outstanding abilities—and who are willing and capable of inheriting and continuing with the company's management philosophy.

Since I am against the hereditary system, employees realize that they all have the potential of rising to the very top of the company. They know that our corporate policies and philosophy are not designed for my own self-benefit. That is why our employees will all follow me even when I demand so much from them.

Workers' attitudes reflect those of the leader.

❧ Deciding to Withdraw ❧

One of the toughest decisions top management ever makes is to withdraw from a project—in other words, where to draw the line if it does not yield enough profit. If we try only for a short while and then quit, we can never achieve good results.

I make it my basic principle to persist until I succeed, just as a hunter goes after game. There have been a few rare times, however, when I have had to withdraw, having exhausted all my ammunition.

Material factors aside, we cannot succeed in any new project or venture without passion. If I see that a project has been pursued until all the passion has burned out, and success is not yet in sight, I am willing to withdraw.

But first we must fight until we have thoroughly exhausted our resources—that is, until passion can no longer be rekindled. At that point, we must decide. Not everything can turn out the way we wish. In some extreme cases, we must know when that time has come and then be capable and willing to make the decision to withdraw.

You must be able to determine the time when it becomes absolutely necessary to withdraw.

A Worthy Task

If your management is poor or misdirected, you can expect your business to go downhill. Even when your management is capable, well meaning, and hard working, circumstances occasionally conspire against you. For example, foreign exchange rates, oil prices, and other factors of international economics are largely beyond our control.

And despite all of your efforts, if external factors force your company to lose money, your management will still be held responsible.

Obviously, an executive responsible for a business bears a very heavy responsibility. You cannot rest your mind for even a moment. You can never reduce your efforts. The more you think about it, the more you may find that being a top executive is not worth all of the stress and demands. Will an executive ever receive a just reward for such responsibility? I believe so!

The dedication of a top executive enables many employees to have hope for today and the future. They trust and respect their employer.

The joy and appreciation of other people can never be measured in monetary terms. This is the greatest compensation any executive could desire.

❧ Strive for Perfection ❧

When it comes to work, I am a perfectionist.

If 90 percent of a task has been accomplished, some people think it is "good enough," and move on. Office workers think they can always delete mistakes with an eraser. Since accomplishing 90 percent of a goal seems pretty good, they seldom pursue *perfection*.

In a chemical experiment, however, a 99 percent success could be totally blown away by the one percent error. Many engineers have been through this battlefield of pursuing the last degree of perfection. They know that even the smallest mistake can be fatal, not just to their project, but perhaps to someone's life. A bridge that *almost* withstands an earthquake has no redeemable value after the disaster. That's why most engineers have an attitude of rigorously pursuing perfection.

It is extremely difficult to begin demanding perfection of yourself in everyday life. However, once it becomes your second nature, you can easily live that way. Aerospace engineers know that it takes tremendous energy to launch a satellite against gravity. But once it is in orbit, the same satellite needs very little energy to remain there.

A business leader must pursue perfection as an everyday habit.

⟨⟨ Light Your Own Way ⟨⟨

In the domain of creativity, there is no standard. It is just like launching a raft onto a dark, stormy ocean without a compass.

During my voyage, when I suffered intense anguish, I desperately sought a lighthouse. But mine was a sea of uncharted territory. There was no lighthouse outside. I had to make a lighthouse of myself to illuminate the way. Being a pioneer means having no path to follow and no one to compete against other than yourself. This realization leads to perfectionism.

"Better" and "best" are terms we use when we have a standard for comparison. "Better" means something is relatively superior to something else; "best" means it is the best *among certain things.* But a pioneer in a new field is like a ship exploring where no one has gone before. As a pioneer, you demand "perfection" of yourself—because you have no one else on whom to rely.

Aiming for perfection also implies that you are on an endless pursuit of your inner ideal.

In the domain of creativity, there is no standard. You have to search for a compass within yourself to determine and pursue your course.

❧ Lead Selflessly ❧

Takamori Nanshuu Saigo, a central figure in Japan's Meiji Restoration, once said: "No one is more unruly than an individual who doesn't desire money, fame, or life. However, I can trust only such an unruly person with important matters of this nation." He would not appoint anyone to a high position unless he was convinced of that person's absolute unselfishness.

There is only one true source of power to influence others, and that is fairness. "Fairness" means that you don't expect any self-benefit and that you make decisions without regard for your own likes or emotions.

It is almost impossible to be immune to the allure of money, fame, or self-preservation. But if you can be a leader who is fair and impartial, your subordinates will follow and respect you. On the other hand, a leader who is self-centered and greedy will be detested.

As a leader, you must clearly indicate your unselfish stand. You should set a meaningful goal for your group and follow it yourself.

The leader's decisions can raise subordinates' spirits or make them sink and suffer. You cannot be temperamental, self-serving, or prone to making decisions for your own convenience, if you expect your subordinates to follow you and not give up.

✌ Question Organization ✌

I have no preset idea of the type of organization we need to run a business.

Most executives do.

They believe they must have a certain type of system because of what they learned in organization theory or personnel management. Or in other cases, they set up an organization based on their past experience. But these preconceptions can never create a truly efficient organization.

I think that the "correct" organization is the one needed to maintain your company and to run it effectively *right now*. Based on this notion, we establish an organization only when we need one, and we assign the minimum number of people necessary to perform each intended function. We don't run a business to support an organization. Rather, we should create the organization we need to run a business.

When I founded my first company, I had neither theoretical knowledge nor experience in managing a business. I even lacked basic business common sense. This left me no choice but to start by questioning every preconceived notion about management.

Manage your business by always asking what is essential, rational, worthwhile, and necessary.

❧ Village Wisdom ❧

Dr. Junichiro Itani, a professor emeritus of Kyoto University and an authority in the study of primates, is a frequent visitor to the Congo region of Africa. He once observed native hunting practices in a small tribal village, and what he witnessed there is quite remarkable.

The people of this village hunted deer and zebra as a group—a method that could easily have provided everyone with more than enough to eat. Yet on each hunting trip, as soon as a single animal could be felled, the entire party would stop hunting and follow the successful hunter proudly back to the village. The game would then be shared according to an apparent rule: after the successful hunter took the best and biggest piece, he would distribute a portion to his close relatives and friends, who in turn shared their portions with their relatives and friends. Everyone got some, and each portion was effectively sized in proportion to how closely related the recipient was to the hunter.

Itani asked one young man why he didn't simply continue hunting until he caught his own deer. The man replied: "Why? My portion was small, but we *did* get enough to eat." He was satisfied to live by the laws of the forest.

To coexist in harmony, no one can be greedy.

❧ A Lesson from Chimpanzees ❧

Chimpanzees are omnivorous. They feed mainly on fruits and leaves, but occasionally, they do hunt and eat meat. They are quite strong, capable of preying on a wide range of other animals.

Like the villagers, chimpanzees also hunt together—and once any one of them kills a large animal, all of the others immediately stop hunting. They gather around the catch, crying out and jumping up and down, as the successful hunter tears it into pieces and shares it with the group.

Chimpanzees are intelligent primates and the closest to humans. Still, it surprised Dr. Itani to find that they hunt within the limit of necessity and purposely live in a way that maintains the chain of regeneration.

When he had previously observed African tribesmen practicing this "one-catch-per-hunt" limit, Itani considered it a primitive custom. He later decided that the tribesmen were following a law of the forest that was more advanced, in many ways, than the practices of "modern" human beings—a law so fundamental, it is followed even by chimpanzees!

In business, as in hunting, selfish practices which seek unlimited expansion will ultimately disrupt the chain of regeneration, and lead to self-destruction.

A Conversation with Kazuo Inamori on Persistence

What is meant specifically by "persistence"?

What I mean is that you must be willing to make "unbeatable" efforts—untiring, constant progress toward a goal despite any amount of hardship or frustration. Each small step you make through such efforts will eventually accumulate into a great feat. Moreover, a person who makes light of minor tasks will never produce a major success. You must be willing to apply yourself to even the smallest tasks with unbeatable efforts.

Is Kyocera unique in emphasizing the value of spirituality in a business? And, if not, can you give us another example of a "spiritual" company?

In 1980, I had the pleasure of meeting with the late Jean Riboud, then the Chairman of Schlumberger. Schlumberger is a French multinational corporation involved in oil exploration services and which at that time, had about 70,000 employees in some 50-odd nations. It was also the new owner of Fairchild Semiconductor, one of our key customers.

During this meeting, Riboud and I discovered that Schlumberger and Kyocera were very similar in that we both placed great emphasis on the importance of having and *believing* in a corporate philosophy that transcends materialism and has quasi-spiritual implications.

I believe this is a trait common to all successful enterprises.

Afterword

I believe that the key to success in business is to exercise a set of moral principles which follow the universal law of leading all living beings to happiness. I also consider it extremely important for individuals to have a pure philosophy.

Please do not consider this book a sermon by a preacher. Rather, I hope that you will ponder upon the principles I have shared in it, and consider using them to develop your own life and business into something even more wonderful than they now are.

About the Author

Dr. Kazuo Inamori, whose management philosophy is shared in this book, is the founder and chairman of both Kyocera and DDI Corporation. He has been named Japan's most outstanding entrepreneur on multiple occasions.

Dr. Inamori was born on January 30, 1932, the second son of a struggling family with seven children, and grew up in the southern prefecture of Kagoshima. At age 27, he and seven colleagues founded Kyoto Ceramic Co. Ltd. with the equivalent of $10,000 in borrowed money. Known today as Kyocera Corporation, the company appears on both the "Fortune 500" (#373 with annual sales of about $4 billion) and the Business Week "Global 1000" (#179 with market valuation of $12 billion).

In 1971, Kyocera became the first Japanese company to establish manufacturing operations in California. Its shares have been traded on the New York Stock Exchange since 1980, and four Americans now sit on its board.

In 1984, Dr. Inamori led 225 other companies to form DDI Corporation, the first and largest privatized telephone company to challenge the monopoly of Nippon Telegraph and Telephone (NTT). As its Chairman, Dr. Inamori directed DDI to form and operate eight reginal cellular telephone subsidiaries in Japan.

In 1993, Kyocera and DDI formed Nippon Iridium. Today, Motorola and Nippon Iridium are the two largest investors in the Iridium Project—a global satellite network which will permit telephone communication between any two points on earth. DDI generated a profit of a half billion dollars on sales of almost four billion dollars and went public the same year.

In 1995, DDI advanced into the emerging personal communications system arena with nine subsidiaries that will offer "pocket" telephone service in every major Japanese city.

Dr. Inamori's personal donation of $200 million in 1984 established the Inamori Foundation and its annual Kyoto Prizes as a way of repaying society for his success. Each year, three prizes representing the categories of Basic Science, Advanced Technology, and Creative Arts and Moral Sciences are awarded to outstanding individuals or groups along with cash awards of approximately $500,000 each. As of the Foundation's 10th anniversary, these prizes have been awarded to 2 Japanese, 16 Europeans and 13 Americans.